# WARNING: The Media May Be Harmful to Your Health! A Consumer's Guide to Medical News and Advertising

# WARNING:
## The Media May Be Harmful to Your Health!
## A Consumer's Guide to Medical News and Advertising

by Ralph C. Heussner, Jr.
    and
Marla E. Salmon

**Andrews and McMeel**

A Universal Press Syndicate Company
Kansas City   •   New York

**Library of Congress Cataloging-in-Publication Data**

Heussner, Ralph C.
  Warning: the media may be harmful to your health!

  Bibliography: p.
  1. Mass media in health education—United States.
2. Advertising—Medicine—United States. 3. Consumer education—United States. I. Salmon, Marla E.
II. Title.
RA440.5.H48   1988     613     88-24241
ISBN 0-8362-2425-6 (pbk.)

# Contents

Preface, *vii*

Acknowledgments, *viii*

Introduction, *ix*

I. **The Modern Medicine Show, 1**

    1. Where Medicine and Media Clash, *3*
    2. Media Constraints and Their Impact
       on Medical News, *15*
    3. Quackery, Flackery, and Hype, *32*

II. **Raising Hopes, Dashing Dreams, Spreading Fear, 43**

    4. Snake Venom and Multiple Sclerosis, *45*
    5. A Dangerous Cure for Cystic Acne, *53*
    6. The Sulindac Seduction, *62*
    7. An "Apocryphal" Tale about Cerebral Palsy, *68*
    8. Selenium Story Put Cystic Fibrosis
       Sufferers at Risk, *72*
    9. Laetrile: Media Hype of Pseudoscience, *78*
    10. Cancer News Coverage, *85*
    11. Herpes Hysteria, *93*
    12. Acupuncture and Hearing Loss, *100*
    13. The Vasectomy Scare, *105*
    14. Sweet News for Diabetics?, *110*
    15. Whooping Cough Makes a Comeback, *116*
    16. Pinwheel Surgery Controversy, *123*
    17. AIDS, *129*
    18. The Charity Campaigns, *135*

### III. How the Press Can Change Your Behavior, 143

19. Media Promotes an "Inebriated Nation," *145*
20. Tobacco Industry's "Switch to Print" Pays Off, *150*
21. Suicides and the "Power of Suggestion," *158*

### IV. The Media as Voyeur, 165

22. The Media and Human Suffering, *167*
23. A Patient's Right to Privacy, *174*

### V. How to Find the Truth, 177

24. A Consumer's Guide to Medical News
    and Advertising, *179*
25. What to Do about Quackery, *187*

### Appendices

I. Publications, *191*
II. Medical Information Hotlines
    and Clearinghouses, *194*
III. A Reporter's Notebook, *196*
IV. Rx for Medical People, *199*
V. The Right Time for Research News, *203*

References, *207*

Index, *217*

# Preface

The news consumer is vulnerable to medical misinformation.

This book attempts to chronicle an area of press behavior that has come under increased criticism during recent years— press coverage of health and medicine. Unlike other books about science and the media, which seek ways to bridge the professional gap between journalists and scientists, this book is written for the consumer of medical information.

Though press criticism has at times been construed as an attempt at regulation, such is not our purpose. Instead, we seek to offer consumers a perspective into the process of medical communication in hopes that their health care decisions will be based on reliable information.

# Acknowledgments

Thanks go to many individuals in a wide range of professions who knowingly and unknowingly made this book possible:

To friends and colleagues in the news business: Roger Capettini, Glen McCutcheon, Bob Wynn, Rich Martin, Rick Beene, Neal St. Anthony, Gainer Bryan, Vic Cohn, Walter Parker, and Lewis Cope;

To University of Minnesota editors and writers: Jeanne Hanson, Lynnette Lamb, Bill Hoffman, Paul Dienhart, Liz Petrangelo, Mary Stanik, and Sharon Farsht;

To scientists and physicians: Henry H. Balfour, Jr., John Kluznik, Kevin Flynn, and Jorge Yunis.

And, most of all, to our respective families: Ralph's wife Carol and son Nathan whose love provides inspiration and energy; and Marla's husband Jerry and children Jessica and Matthew, who somehow keep on giving even when it seems impossible to give more.

# Introduction

"Don't trust what you read in health and diet books," warned Mark Twain. "You might die of a misprint."

Although Twain's comment was voiced nearly a century ago, it conveys wisdom that is equally relevant to health messages appearing in the print and electronic media of today. But the problem is far graver than simple misprints. Consumers must be wary of misinformation caused by sensational or incomplete news reporting and misleading advertising.

The process of communicating medical information is seriously flawed. Because the system lacks safeguards to protect the public from gullible reporters, entrepreneurial scientists, profit-minded medical manufacturers, and quacks, the consumer should be suspect of most health messages conveyed via the news media. The news media can be harmful to your health unless you are prepared to resist its messages. Like a nefarious disease, the press is capable of doing harm in many way:

• Irresponsible and sensational medical reporting can hurt a patient's physical and psychological well-being. By touting preliminary or unusual research that raises hopes of the sick and dying, the press sometimes diverts patients from conventional and proven therapies. Desperate patients are tempted to put their hopes in new, unproven "cures." As newspapers and electronic media place more emphasis on health news, they inadvertently have become purveyors of health hype. Media competition has meant that some reporters now go public with unproven medical research in order to be "first" with the story, known in journalism as a "scoop." A survey of twenty-seven leading American science journalists found that the "dominant distorting influence" in science journalism was the "competitive force" that "creates a tension between the incentive for reporters to hype a story and a counterdesire to maintain credibility," says Jay Winsten, director of the Office of Health Policy Information at the Harvard School of Public Health.[1]

• By permitting alcohol and tobacco manufacturers to advertise their products, the media promote behavior that shortens people's lives and increases their risk of cancer, heart disease, emphysema, and a long list of other maladies. There is evidence that some news organizations either downplay or ignore news stories because of financial pressures of advertisers.

• The press is pernicious because it invades people's privacy. A patient who undergoes the first-of-a-kind surgery or receives the latest life-saving drug will be hounded by reporters demanding a personal account of the experience and details about the family's finances. If the patient's condition worsens, the press holds a "death watch," sometimes camping out in a hospital's lobby to await the story's final episode.

• The portrayal of aberrant behavior in news and feature programming has resulted in imitative behavior—and an increase in violence and suicides.

• Finally, scare stories about alleged public health hazards have given the public a distorted understanding of the actual extent of the danger. As a result, some sick individuals, including school children with herpes or AIDS, have been unjustly ostracized and harassed because of public hysteria caused by fear-provoking news accounts. The press also tends to exaggerate the extent of some public health problems, such as the prevalence of toxic-shock syndrome and Legionnaires' disease.

## Who Should Read This Book?

This book is relevant for three audiences. The book is primarily aimed at lay people—curious consumers—who will gain a healthy skepticism toward medical news reports and advertisements appearing in the press. Second, neophyte reporters may learn from the past experiences of their predecessors. Finally, this book will interest physicians, scientists, and other health practitioners who are the subject of medical news stories.

## An Overview of the Problem

Why are the popular media saturated with medical messages? Several factors contribute to the recent emphasis on medical breakthroughs and bulging advertising budgets for the promotion of health care. First, the biomedical revolution has spawned myriad new drugs, devices, and ways of manipulating the body to fight disease. The revolution in treatment has followed a knowledge explosion. At the same time, doctors and hospitals are facing the challenge of competition, thus forcing a new emphasis on marketing and public relations to get the word out to the public. In some cases, the press has become a pawn in the frenzied marketing of health care.

To keep pace with the medical revolution, news organizations have responded by assigning reporters with little or no medical education to translate complex scientific findings into layman's language. Some major newspapers devote weekly sections to science and medical news. The media's commitment to cover medicine has pressured reporters to develop interesting and provocative stories. Some reporters have become overly anxious to report the latest medical development, resulting in exaggeration or oversimplification.

All reporters face problems of accuracy and selectivity, but these problems are magnified in medical reporting because errors and sensationalism in stories about potentially curative potents have more direct impact on human life. Professor R. Gordon Shepherd, a sociologist at the University of Central Arkansas, writes: "The translation of scientific work and its implications for lay audiences involve great potential for sheer inaccuracy through reporters' inability to interpret their subject correctly, or their propensity to oversimplify, or both. News distortion or 'refraction' produced through selectivity is, if anything, potentially more serious."[2]

Why are these errors so grievous to the news consumer?

• For a large segment of the American public, the popular press—newspapers, television, and radio—is their sole source of medical information. A story or advertisement in these news outlets may be their only exposure to the story. They are particularly vulnerable to misinformation.

• Acutely ill and dying patients have a natural hope that medicine will, in time, heal them. They may read more into the story or advertisement than what is really there.

• Stories about experimental drugs and treatments can lead patients away from conventional therapy that works. In some cases, patients and their families waste precious time and money chasing an obscure and bogus therapy.

• Medical information is more complex and subject to more errors of understanding and interpretation.

• The nature of the news business is such that "firsts" receive the most exhaustive and extensive coverage. Even though the second drug on the market might be better, it won't attract the same kind of media attention as the first because by then it's considered "old news."

• Reporters often fail to appreciate the impact of their words and pictures on those who suffer.

But journalists are not always at fault. Sometimes, physicians and scientists are guilty of jumping to conclusions about the significance of their work. They may go public with their findings before verification or review by other experts. Finally, manufacturers of medical products may embellish the merits of their new drug or device in order to get publicity.

This book does not claim that every medical story is inaccurate, overplayed, or sensational. Nor do we contend that the purpose of every medical advertisement is to bilk the consumer. But the medically unsophisticated consumer cannot judge when information is accurate. Even well-educated laypeople are unable to evaluate the signficance of the latest medical development. Therefore, the public is at the mercy of a reporter interpreting the complexities of medical science, or the copywriter preparing the advertisement.

Maverick scientists, overly optimistic physicians, and zealous medical device manufacturers are all capable of leading the press astray. Quacks can sometimes interest reporters in writing about their magic potion. If they can't get publicity in the news columns, there is always the paid advertising route.

Besides the press, there is another fallible component in the communication equation. The receiver of information may exercise poor judgment by reading too much significance into the story; small advances take on a larger meaning. Some news consumers may simply block out the important qualifiers because they hear what they want to hear and believe what they want to believe. The mind can be gullible and unreliable. This is especially true when a family member is touched by an incurable illness. So besides questioning the message and the medium, news consumers must doubt themselves.

## How This Book Is Organized

Part I examines various conflicts between medicine and the media. Where do medical stories originate? Why does one scientific study whet the news media's appetite and not another? Can the press be manipulated by irreputable scientists? Has the recent emphasis on health care marketing spawned a new kind of medical quackery?

Part II presents fifteen examples of how sensational, ill-timed, or erroneous news reporting has raised the hopes of people falsely, or led them away from conventional treatments based on preliminary research results of new therapies. The final chapter in this section, "The Charity Campaigns," scrutinizes the media's role in fund-raising for experimental operations and questions whether only "mediagenic" children get help.

Part III looks at the press as a behavior modifier. Have news editors shied away from covering the tobacco link to cancer because they fear that their publication will lose lucrative advertising? What is the relationship between alcohol beverage advertising and alcoholism? A chapter in this section discusses recent research that indicates that press reporting of suicides results in an increase in suicide deaths, especially among teenagers, in the period immediately after the press coverage.

Part IV probes the role of the press as a social voyeur. Voyeurism is a word used more frequently to describe the act of deriving sexual pleasure from viewing the intimate aspects of others lives. We have applied the word to the news media which derives pleasure and professional gain by invading the privacy of patients who become "newsworthy."

Part V gives readers a guidebook through the medical information maze. How can laypeople interpret medical research? The major problem for the consumer, whose life may depend on the words in newsprint or the comments on TV, is deciding when to accept the latest medical discovery. We contend that all medical news should be viewed skeptically. You don't require a graduate degree in the biological sciences to put "new medicine" into perspective. A wise news consumer can become medically well-informed. This is no easy task because medical information is fragmentary, contradictory, and complex. This book will help you through the quagmire.

# I The Modern Medicine Show

What makes medical news? How accurate are news stories about medical advances that appear in the popular press? Where do reporters find information about the latest medical breakthrough? What causes tension between medical practitioners and medical reporters? Can the press be manipulated by quacks and other medical hypsters? In this section, we examine these and other questions about the inherent conflicts between medicine and the news media.

# 1 Where Medicine and Media Clash

"The world today is divided into two conceptual groups—the scientist and the nonscientist—and the communication gap between them is wide and serious."

—Daniel E. Koshland, Jr., editor of *Science*[1]

One reason for the gap is that scientists (including physicians and medical researchers) and nonscientists don't communicate directly; messages are processed through the news media. Journalists are filters through which the public receives and digests medical information. The filtering process is fraught with hazards because medicine and the press have different rules, languages, and outlooks on the world. These differences lead to misinterpretation, sensationalism, omission, oversimplification, and distortion in the dissemination of medical news. Here's a look at several areas of conflict.

## A Fight for Control

A natural tension exists whenever the two professions collide. The tension often is caused by divergent views of what is important or newsworthy. For example, in defining accuracy, the science editor of the now-defunct *Chicago Daily News* once noted the following difference: "Whereas science is accurate to ten decimal points, newspapers like to settle for round figures."[2]

3

Scientists adhere to strict statistical criteria when presenting information. Their work is subject to rigorous professional critique called "peer review," meaning it must be read, evaluated and verified by other specialists before it is published in a journal. On the other hand, the reporter's story, which will reach a larger public in a very short time frame, is reviewed by one or two editors, who usually have less experience in the medical field than the reporter.

Another reason for the tension is the question of control. When scientists publish results of their work in scientific journals, they are responsible for what is written. But when a reporter takes the information and "translates" it for the nonscientific audience, the reporter becomes the responsible author. "No matter how careful the researcher is, how many times he or she qualifies things, how many times he or she goes back over things, there's nothing a researcher can do to control what that reporter is going to say," writes Dr. Robert DuPont, clinical professor of psychiatry at Georgetown School of Medicine.[3]

## Jaded Objectivity

The popular press seeks to find truth by airing divergent views on a subject. In presenting two perspectives on a new medical discovery with equal credibility, each is given equal space, even if 99 percent of researchers in the field agree and only 1 percent disagrees. For example, when the American Psychiatric Association voted to eliminate homosexuality from its inventory of mental illnesses, at least one major American daily newspaper felt obliged to include a comment in its story from a clinician who still believed the sexual practice was a "disgusting perversion."[4]

A patient who believes in a quack cure may be placed on an equal plane with a physician who has devoted a lifetime of study aimed at disproving hoax medications. Truth, in the journalist's view, is for the impartial news consumer to decide. In medicine, "objective" is not a reconciliation of opinions, but rather conclusions made from hard facts derived by the scientific method.

A study of biomedical innovation and the press by two Stanford University researchers—one a professor in the School of Medicine and the other a writer in the Public Affairs Office—found that press coverage was not very objective at all and was often either pro-industry or sensationalized. Nancy Pfund and Laura Hofstadter wrote in the *Journal of Communication:*

> Media coverage of recombinant DNA and the biomedical research often paralleled the industry point of view, with uneven attention to views of dissident scientists or to events not prepackaged for consumption.
>
> The general political climate and inclinations of reporters . . . often resulted in coverage that favored splash over substance and events over implications.
>
> Many articles fail to provide a scientific context for reported discoveries. Key questions are repeatedly left unanswered, including whether or not results have been published, or whether or not researchers made a product with actual biological activity. Often these questions are not even asked.[5]

## Different Time Zones

By and large, medical science proceeds in a tortoise-like fashion. Knowledge advances in small, incremental steps—not in great leaps. But the press has a tendency to treat new developments as "breakthroughs" that occur suddenly, thanks to the achievements of only one or a few people.

Medical science begins with a hypothesis or idea, followed by time-consuming experiments where tedious attention is given to detail. Then there is publication in peer-reviewed journals, and finally verification by other scientists before the hypothesis is accepted as truth.

Before medical scientists can produce a cure, they must understand the cause of the disease. For example, Jonas Salk received the lion's share of credit in the popular press for inventing the polio vaccine. Press reports focused on Salk, as if he had discovered it all by himself. But, in the view of many medical historians, the real heroes were the researchers who conducted the basic experiments, which involved growing the polio virus in a monkey kidney. Their work made the human vaccine possible, and they eventually won the Nobel Prize—not Salk—though their work was largely ignored by the press, and their names never became known to the public.[6]

Scientists and journalists have different publication deadlines. "Sometimes I don't even have the luxury of 10 minutes to get a story out," says Warren Leary, Associated Press (AP) science writer. "We are more or less composing and thinking about a story as we are dictating it over a telephone."[7] Publication in a medical journal—the accepted forum for disseminating new discoveries to the scientific community—takes months.

The pure scientist tends to resist releasing study findings until the evidence has passed through the gamut of the peer review process, meaning that it has been evaluated and substantiated by other researchers in the field. This process requires much time—sometimes years—to verify results. Reporters, on the other hand, work against daily or weekly deadlines. They are under constant pressure to produce instant analyses of the impact of new medical findings on the public. The journalist often wants to tell the story before there is a consensus of experts. Reporters frequently quote patients whose objectivity is suspect because of their inherent desire to improve.

When are the results of medical research ready for public consumption? Journalists and physicians/scientists have clashed over the question for years without a clear resolution. Their respective arguments run like this:

*The Journalist Point of View:* Most journalists believe that medical research is news at almost any stage—the awarding of the grant, the laboratory work, the animal experiment, the human trials, or the Food and Drug Administration (FDA) approval. It's news if reporters are able to make sense of the research and put it into language and context that their audience will understand. They believe that because of the First Amendment right guaranteeing freedom of the press, and the fact that most medical research is government subsidized, there should be no locks on the door to medical information.

*The Physician/Scientist Point of View:* Most scientists contend medical research results should not be made public before they have been evaluated and confirmed by their peers. Hypotheses and animal studies should be ignored because of their preliminary nature. To publicize this work prematurely could lead patients astray and raise their hopes unrealistically.

The following example illustrates how these philosophies clash in the real world of medical journalism.

In April 1981, a pioneering surgical procedure on an unborn human fetus took place at University of Colorado Hospital in Denver. The fetus was diagnosed with hydrocephalus, a buildup of fluid around the brain. To correct the deformity, surgeons implanted a thin tube into the brain to drain fluid, allowing the brain to return to its normal size. Hydrocephalic swelling can cause extreme mental retardation, and, in some cases, death.

About a month after the operation, *Denver Post* reporter Bill Symons learned of the operation from a source he called "unimpeachable." Symons contends that he tried for a month to gain official confirmation of the surgery, but hospital authorities refused to make any statement.

In June, the newspaper advised the two physicians involved in the surgery that it planned to go ahead and publish a story without their confirmation. According to Symons, "Points we weighed included the fact that the medical center is university affiliated, with a large portion of its funding coming from state taxes and federal research grants."[8]

To protest a "no comment response" from the hospital and physicians, the newspaper filed a grievance with the Code of Cooperation Committee of the Colorado Hospital Association, which was composed of news-media representatives, hospital administrators, public relations people, and a physician. In its review of the incident, the committee found that the physicians were in violation of the Code of Cooperation because the patient had become a "public figure" by virtue of the unique surgical procedure.

The doctors argued strongly against publication on grounds that the stories might jeopardize the patient's right to privacy. They were also concerned that the experimental procedure might give false hopes to families of potential patients. After all, there was no assurance that the surgery was successful. The doctors said they also wanted to publish their work in a medical journal where it would draw comment from other physicians.

In response to the newspaper's action, the doctors wrote in a letter to the *New England Journal of Medicine* in the February 4, 1982, issue that "the experience has pointed out that the press feels free to disregard the patient's right to privacy and the right of investigators to release their story at the time and in the place of their own choosing."

From the press standpoint, "news is news." It was unthinkable to wait for publication in the scientific literature, which takes several months. But from the scientist's perspective, the medical journal is the appropriate method for releasing information. (The Colorado physicians eventually published a detailed account of the procedure in *The New England Journal of Medicine.*)

## Competition Leads to Scoop Journalism

The popular press is a business. To survive in the highly competitive market, a news outlet requires interesting and dramatic stories if it is to find and keep a loyal audience. Medical stories, therefore, must be written and packaged to whet the information appetites of the consumers.

This competition means reporters are pressured to be first with a medical story, or at least to come up with a fresh angle on it. Information is gathered, packaged, and published according to the next deadline—for daily newspapers and television stations the cycle is repeated every twenty-four hours. In the case of fast-breaking events, stories often go out before the facts are double-checked with other medical authorities. The doctor may be in surgery, examining patients, or consulting with other physicians on a complicated case, and therefore unable to respond to a reporter's inquiry.

## Defining Newsworthiness?

What is significant to the medical reporter isn't always viewed as important by physicians and scientists. For example, the press considers an anecdotal story about a patient's recovery legitimate news for publication or broadcast. Scientists see little relevance in a single patient's response; they look for trends that are "statistically significant."

The two professions also differ in the manner of presentation. Scientific material usually consists of dry facts, presented in a tedious and complicated format. The news media prefer a more general presentation of a scientific study, sometimes before it is proven.

Nathan S. Haseltine, a distinguished science writer at the *Washington Post* and *Times Herald* for many years, wrote of this problem:

> Newspapermen and physicians live in their own worlds. They see the same things, but each views them from his own training.
>
> The newspaperman looks on something new as news, something competitive which he must write about before his fellow newspapermen. If it is a promising medical development which doesn't pan out, that's all right, too. The stories of failures are the pegs on which he hangs later newspaper stories.
>
> When the doctor sees something new—except perhaps when he has developed it himself—he sees something that is yet to be proved. He may see its promises, but until they have been fulfilled he is leery of such claims.[9]

Controversy adds spice to journalism. Controversial stories are more likely to receive better "play"—a press term for prominent display in the newspaper, one of the incentives of the news business. Other factors that make a story newsworthy include: the number of individuals potentially affected by a news development and whether it is unique, such as the first-of-a-kind operation.

## Language Barriers

Medical science, as well as other technological fields, has developed a language of its own. In medical jargon or "argot," words may carry a different meaning than when they're transmitted to the public. For example, the word "discovery" is often interpreted by the journalist as a breakthrough whereas the scientist uses the term to describe the process of gathering data.

Medical writers for the popular press use colorful, casual, everyday language to create interest and help understanding among a non-medical audience. Popular writers frequently use analogies and similes to explain ideas unfamiliar to the lay reader. Scientists, on the other hand, employ a precise and technical language, usually written in the passive tense with lots of statistics. Because the scientist often deals with abstract concepts, information is dry, impersonal, and not obviously relevant to the everyday lives of the public.

Like interpreting a foreign language, the translation process of science has inherent problems. Jo Ann Shroyer, former medical and science reporter for Minnesota Public Radio, says scientists use "careful talk" when expressing themselves while reporters write and report in "straight talk" to communicate with their news consumers. Shroyer writes:

> Reporters are in a never-ending quest for real language. Careful talk drifts over us like a Thanksgiving snowstorm that we must sift for meaning. Straight talk, and that jewel in the crown of newsmakers, colorful talk, leap out at us. . . . Some plain talk would make reporters' jobs easier and help the public understand how one study fits into the big picture, but because of careful talk and the misunderstandings it can cause, the public becomes suspicious of all research studies, some researchers become wary of reporters, and reporters despair of ever getting it right.[10]

Language problems occur partly because of perspective. Such was the case a few years ago when a University of Minnesota surgeon complained about the use of the word "experimental" in a story about pancreas transplants as a treatment for diabetes.[11] From the reporter's perspective, the word was probably intended to emphasize its preliminary status and not raise the hopes of people. But the researcher said he had never used the word in the interview because "the word makes it sould like I'm experimenting on people, like you do on animals." Instead of "experimental," the researcher said he had used the word "developmental" during the interview. To the scientist, the word conveys a process; to the lay public, it means little.

## Missing Qualifiers

The fact that medical science doesn't deal in absolutes frustrates journalists. Because no drug or surgical procedure always works, physicians must qualify what they say in both publications and oral communication with patients and the press. These uncertainties result in the use of qualifiers—words such as "may," "if," "but," and "perhaps." To the scientist, these words quarantee a safety net in the event that the medical advance doesn't work. They make the journalist's job difficult.

Dr. Lauren A. Woods, vice president for Health Sciences at Virginia Commonwealth University, gives the following example of how a drug's effect might be misinterpreted by reporters because of a scientist's cautious use of words.

Suppose I were to say that drug X has a positive inotropic effect on heart muscle. To some of you this might mean something. But to most laymen and many scientists, it would be more meaningful to say that this drug helps a weakened heart to pump blood. Now let me carry this illustration a little bit farther. I will say Y amount of this drug will correct the failure of the heart in a given patient. Will that hold true for every patient with heart failure given Y amount of a specific drug? No, it won't and here are the reasons: there are different kinds of heart patients; some types will not respond to this drug. In addition, there is biological variation; that is, Y amounts of the drug in another patient may not have the same effect. Reporters so often want the question answered yes or no as to when a selected chemical or drug is supposed to have a given effect. Under certain conditions, a chemical or drug will have a given effect; under others, it will not. Very often a scientist cannot answer simply yes or no. Based on his experience and knowledge, he has to provide qualified answers.[12]

A missing qualifier caused considerable confusion following a study of the drug Acyclovir at the University of Minnesota. In 1981, researchers announced that the drug was effective in treating shingles, a common ailment of the elderly. But the study showed the drug was effective only if given within three days of the onset of the rash. The story received widespread media attention throughout the country, but some news reports failed to mention that the drug must be given "within three days." Hundreds of shingles patients, including many suffering lingering pain called postherpetic neuralgia, had their hopes raised only to be told upon inquiry that the drug was not for them. Here's what *USA Today* said in its June 16, 1981 edition:

> A drug recently approved to treat genital herpes can also help clear up shingles, a skin infection, says a report in today's New England Journal of Medicine. The drug Acyclovir helped prevent spread of the infection, caused by a virus called herpes zoster, in 94 people whose immune systems were not functioning properly. About 500,000 Americans develop shingles each year. It is especially prevalent, and can be life threatening, among those past age 60 and in people whose immune systems are malfunctioning due to cancer and other disease, says Dr. Henry H. Balfour, Jr., of the University of Minnesota Health Sciences Center, Minneapolis, who directed the study. "This is definitely an effective treatment for shingles," he said.[13]

## Uncredible Sources

Most journalists have limited education and training in medicine. Therefore, they cannot reach independent conclusions regarding the value of a new drug, surgical treatment, or biomechanical device. To explain the latest medical invention, the journalist must rely on "experts." The expert can be anyone who boasts of an advanced degree, even those whose "expertise" comes from degrees obtained from questionable institutions. The press may use patients' comments to explain medical discoveries.

According to *Science in the Streets*, a 1984 review of media coverage of health risks by the charitable organization Twentieth Century Fund:

> Unlike an expert witness in a courtroom, those designated as experts by the media do not have to possess specific qualifications to face the media and is all but immune from critical scrutiny and tends to acquire enhanced credibility from the frequency with which he is quoted—and that usually depends on his ability to say things sharply and succinctly, but not necessarily accurately.[14]

# 2 Media Constraints and Their Impact on Medical News

Medicine is front page news. Hardly a day goes by without several medical articles appearing in major newspapers and on television news. Reporters are hungry for stories about medicine because their editors and news directors display them prominently. Editors do so because marketing consultants have found that the public craves stories about "the miracles of modern medicine."

For news consumers, stories about medical progress provide welcome relief from the daily deluge of "bad news." Medical stories often contain a dramatic element—the heroics of physicians or a dying patient's fight for life—that makes the tale even more gripping.

Franz J. Ingelfinger, the late editor of the *New England Journal of Medicine*, wrote: "Until about 1960, the lay press paid little heed to what doctors knew and what they did, and, with rare exceptions, medically related stories were quietly noted on some back page of the paper."[1] A review of the *New York Times* index of subjects is one barometer of the inflationary index for medical news. In 1950, the newspaper carried five pages of citations for health stories; that increased to twenty-five pages in 1975.

If the public thirsts for medical news, the medical community certainly has a lot to tell them—and many physicians and scientists willing to spread the word. "Being a medical reporter today is much easier than when I started twenty years ago," says a veteran big city newspaperman. "Whereas getting doctors to talk to you back then was like pulling teeth, today my desk is covered by news releases, phone messages from PR people and even letters from doctors and researchers who want me to write stories about their work. They want the free publicity."

## The Process of Science Communication

How does a medical story find its way into the lay press? Why do some new developments receive massive attention, while others get only a scant mention in newspapers and other media—even when medical journals express widespread interest in a subject? The answers are complex. News decisions are made based on personal interests of reporters and editors, competition from other media, the promotion abilities of scientists and their sponsors, and current events of the day. (For example, a new drug for arthritis may be front page news on a slow news day, but relegated to an inside page if a passenger jet crashes or if a well-known politician is involved in a criminal act.) To understand why some medical stories attract news coverage, one must first understand the process of communication.

Medical stories, just like other news items in newspapers, radio, and TV, pass through a series of communication channels before they reach the news consumer. The channels are sometimes controlled by gatekeepers who know little or nothing about medicine and the significance of a new medical development.

The process begins with "informants." These are people from special interest groups, individual citizens who want the media to cover a story of concern to them, and public relations people, whose job it is to tout the work of their employer, such as hospitals, medical schools, or medical manufacturers. The informants may lure a medical writer through a news release, a press conference, or a simple phone call. A reporter may choose to develop a story because of a personal interest in the subject, in which case he or she seeks out the informant or source.

After preparing the story, the reporter must deal with a series of editors ("gatekeepers") who may require changes in both content and writing style. They include a news editor who decides where the article will be "played"—meaning where it will be positioned in the newspaper or telecast—and a copy editor who writes the headline and may even rewrite the story.

Judgments about the significance of a particular story occur at every step along this chain. If a PR person believes a story has major news appeal, a news conference may be held in order to draw maximum media attention. If a news editor thinks a story will be read or viewed by a large enough audience, it may be placed on page one of the newspaper or at the top of the television newscast.

In all media, space and time are precious commodities. Therefore, the medical story must be tightly packaged to conform to these constraints. Details about how experiments were done and the qualifying quotes of scientists may have to be deleted if the story is to make it into print. Because of deadlines, there may not be time to double check with the reporter or his sources when a story has been rewritten on the copy desk.

Radio and television are more prone to errors of omission simply because of the nature of electronic media. News stories must be brief, simple, and lively with attention-grabbing pictures to keep the audience tuned in. Rarely are stories long enough to explain a medical story in depth. Television tends to overplay stories with good pictures, and underplay other stories because of their lack of visuals.

Ron Powers, media critic for CBS, has described television's limitations in science coverage as follows:

> In the vacuum of any coherent structure for covering science, the networks are vulnerable to all sorts of unnecessary embarassments. They are prey to the assaults of the self interested public relations manipulations, as in the outrageous stonewalling by the doctors at Loma Linda, where Baby Fae lay dying with her baboon-heart transplant. They can be seduced by the enthusiasm of mob journalism to overreport "success stories" such as last October's (1984) false heralding of a triumph over Alzheimer's disease at Dartmouth-Hitchcock Medical Center. They tend to overidealize the work and the motivations of surgeons while ignoring the less glamorous—and endangered—contributions of pure scientific research.[2]

## Where Does Medical News Originate?

Where do reporters find stories about medicine?

Every year, thousands of medical studies are published by legitimate researchers in the United States and abroad, yet only a small fraction will gain the attention of the mass media, which in turn, informs the public about "medical progress." Even the most well-read medical scientist cannot keep abreast of every major development.

So how does a medical reporter choose which stories to pursue? The answer is twofold: the subject matter of newspaper articles and electronic reports may result from the personal whims of the reporter who finds a subject interesting, ·or the story may be manufactured through manipulation of the press by those who seek to have it tell a story for purposes of education, promotion, or profit. The sources may be hospitals looking for publicity to boost falling patient census, a patient trying to raise money for an experimental operation, a researcher lobbying for grant support, a scientist-entrepreneur who wants to interest venture capitalists, or, sometimes, the quack.

## The Reporter's World

Before scrutinizing these various sources of medical news, the nonjournalist should understand several constraints governing medical reporters. First, unlike other reporters who are able to observe an event firsthand—such as a fire or political rally—the medical reporter usually relies on "secondhand" information from other sources.

As professor Warren Burkett of the University of Texas at Austin explains, "Science writers are rarely present at the making of scientific news."[3] Because very few medical writers have medical backgrounds, they cannot interpret the significance of a medical story themselves; they must rely on the ability of physicians and scientists to articulate its meaning and importance. Medical writers define their function as one of a bridge between the researcher or physician and the average citizen.

Sometimes, the press acts as a conveyor belt, simply carrying the latest "medical news" without questioning study results or examining the qualifications of the news source. Many medical reporters stand in awe of the medical profession. This implicit faith has resulted in the failure to critically analyze some medical developments. One medical journalist has described press vulnerability this way: "We are simply conduits of information. If a doctor or scientist says this is important, who am I to say it isn't?"

Good medical reporters do exist; a few have earned the respect and admiration of the scientific community. They include veteran newsmen such as Victor Cohn of the *Washington Post*, David Pearlman of the *San Francisco Chronicle*, Lewis Cope of the *Minneapolis Star & Tribune*, and Jane Brody and Walter Sullivan of the *New York Times*. But it isn't always the experienced reporter who covers the story. Smaller news outlets, which can't afford a medical reporter specialist, have an even harder time presenting an accurate account of the news. It is a gift to be able to walk gracefully through both the world of medicine and the domain of journalism. As the executive editor of the *Detroit News* once remarked, "A good medical reporter takes years to develop."[4] In the meantime, the public must suffer.

The other news selection factor that sometimes distorts the news is the professional reward system of the news media. Reporters succeed in a larger news organization by producing stories that are featured prominently. Medical reporters must compete with other reporters for scarce space or air time. A medical story with drama and impact is more likely to get better "play," meaning that it will be placed on the front page of the newspaper or promoted and featured as the top story on the six o'clock newscast.

Although most journalists strive to present an "objective" and truthful account of an event, objectivity, according to University of Indiana journalism professor J. Albert Altschull, "is as slippery as an eel; no matter how you seize it, it is difficult to hold on to it."[5] Objectivity requires that the reporter first understand the significance of a medical development, then be able to explain in words or pictures that are relevant to news consumers. If medical reporters are not present at the scene of medical discovery, then where do they find information about it? And how accurate are these sources?

News media organizations allow reporters great latitude in developing stories, especially on the medical beat, which is extremely specialized. Few editors are qualified to question the veracity of the medical reporter's story. Patrick Young, science writer for the Newhouse News Service, explained: "How do I select a story? First, it's got to appeal to me. I've got to be awfully interested in a topic before I'm going to write about it. The next consideration is what's going to bring a certain story or topic into print. Essentially, it's hitting me with the sense, 'Gee, I didn't know that,' or 'Gee, that's interesting,' or 'I haven't seen anything on that.' "[6]

## The Medical Meeting

Most major medical organizations hold annual meetings where clinicians and researchers gather to discuss new findings, review emerging therapies, and resolve current medical debates. Often, the group will discuss financial and ethical questions. Surgeons have their own meetings, as do infectious disease experts, ophthalmologists, and other specialists.

Too often the medical meeting is a prime source of news for medical reporters. The meeting offers reporters an opportunity to meet scientists in a comfortable setting, away from the hospital ward or laboratory, with ready-made topics presented daily. But how important and accurate are the reports emanating from scientific meetings? And are reporters covering the most important topics of the day?

There are several problems with news stories based on scientific meetings. First, research presented here is very preliminary and does not undergo the same strict peer review that attends articles published in medical journals. Second, the presentations are usually brief—ten to fifteen minutes— and concentrate more on methods than results. Third, the presentation is not geared for the general public nor intended to rally patient interest. The presenter is speaking to his or her peers, soliciting their questions and advice; the presentation may be intended as stimulus for future dialogue or more research. Thus, the speaker is likely to be more candid or exaggerate the implications (with the caveat that more study is imperative before accepting the theory), unaware of the medical reporter's presence in the audience.

Many medical and science organizations actively solicit press coverage in hopes of improving the public perception of their work. Press conferences may be arranged to publicize some research and give visibility to the organization. Reporters find it difficult to ignore a major medical meeting, especially if a topic of interest has a widespread public interest, such as AIDS or organ transplantation. Some medical meetings can attract as many as a hundred journalists, resulting in the "pack mentality" approach to medical news coverage. Even seasoned medical reporters with a distaste for publicizing early results are pressured into preparing a story because of the competition.

How reliable is the information presented in abstract form at a medical meeting? Will it eventually be published, thus becoming part of the permanent record of science? To find out, Dr. Lee Goldman and Anita Loscalzo of Harvard Medical School followed a randomly selected group of 276 abstracts presented at the American College of Cardiology Scientific Session of the 1976 meeting. They determined that after more than three years of follow-up, barely half of the abstracts had appeared as full-length articles in peer-reviewed journals.[7] Presumably, the unpublished papers were either unimportant or flawed and, thus, rejected. Some of the papers may have been modified to the point that the MEDLARS (Medical Literature Analysis and Retrieval System of the National Library of Congress) search system was unable to detect the original abstract.

Although 59 percent of the papers were ultimately published, a clear message emerged from the study: medical reporters should ignore or play down preliminary reports. As *New England Journal of Medicine* editor Arnold S. Relman commented: "In their headlong rush to get the latest research 'news' into print, reporters covering clinical meetings may often be doing the public a disservice. It is difficult enough to interpret for the public medical research that has been reviewed and published in full. Where is the virtue in publicizing work that may never even merit scientific publication?"[8]

## Scanning Medical Journals

Many reporters subscribe to medical journals as a source for story ideas. But in scanning the pages of the medical journals, reporters tend to pick up curiosities, way-out ideas, or anything to do with the popular disease of the day. They often ignore the more relevant, yet less dramatic medical advances. The story that gets reported to the general public is sometimes chosen according to the whims of a reporter.

Although publication in a peer-reviewed scientific journal means that medical research has some legitimacy, it by no means insures the ultimate truth of the finding. David Pearlman, associate editor and science editor of the *San Francisco Chronicle* and one of the most respected science writers in America, gives the following example:

> I prefer very much when I'm talking about research results to wait until there's been some form of peer review, although certainly that's no guarantee of validity or significance. I remember covering a surgeon's meeting at which a paper was presented about the "miracle" of gastric freezing for ulcers. The paper was published in a well-reviewed medical journal. A year later the same surgical team from the Midwest appeared before the same surgical meeting to announce that [the procedure] didn't work at all. Even the most prestigious journal can be wrong.[9]

Scientific journals acknowledge that they cannot assure the veracity of every article. In cases of controversial research, some journals will carry editorial comment on the article that attempts to put it in perspective. For example, a few years ago *Scientific Monthly* featured an article by a physician on the effect of low-level radiation on health. He claimed to have found a link between medical x-rays and the risk of leukemia and heart disease. An AP reporter interviewed the physician and the story appeared in hundreds of media outlets across the country. Missing from the AP dispatch was any mention of an editorial note in the same issue of the magazine that stated the article was being published without peer review and that the author of the story stands "virtually alone in the defense of his data." In the same issue of the journal was a rebuttal by two cancer specialists that also went unmentioned. Several days after the sensational story, AP issued a follow-up "explanation."[10]

**Biased News Releases**

Journalists are flooded with handouts—news releases—about medicine. They come from myriad sources: hospitals, medical societies, medical schools, foundations, and even individual medical researchers who seek publicity in the popular press. The news release is usually prepared by a public relations representative in consultation with the medical "expert." The PR person then distributes the release to the press at large, hoping to catch the interest of some reporters.

Because the news release is designed to generate positive publicity, it rarely tells the whole story and sometimes tends to "stretch the truth" in order to attract news interest. For example, a drug company may either leave out or downplay the side effects of a new drug in its news release. A university scientist seeking publicity about his cancer research may ignore similar work conducted at other institutions. While veteran medical reporters view news releases as merely a "news tip," small-town newspapers and television and radio are likely to use them verbatim, without checking any deeper into the story.

### The Pavlovian Press Conference

The press conference is a popular format for the release of medical information. It works like this: an institution or hospital has some "news" that, in the eyes of either the institution or the scientist, is important and deserves widespread dissemination. Rather than simply sending out a news release in the hope the press will use the story, a press conference is called to bring the journalists onto home turf. The press conference may pressure a reticent reporter into covering a story because of the competition. It often results in "mob journalism" behavior where the mere presence of many media people give an event news significance.

A press conference also pressures the reporter to get the story on the evening news or into the next day's newspaper, thus precluding efforts to substantiate the findings that are announced. Because not all press conferences coincide with publication of a study, the comments may be based on opinion or speculation of the researchers, rather than study results or hard data. Unlike information that goes into a medical journal, there is no peer review or editing of a scientist who talks directly to the press.

Most researchers will encounter medical reporters only occasionally during their careers. Therefore, they are at an immediate disadvantage when facing TV cameras and the barrage of questions at the news conference. Basic researchers will be pressed to explain and possibly inflate their work to the clinical setting, e.g., questions like "Doctor, how will your discovery lead to better treatment for patients?" It is human nature to be cooperative and to answer questions. A curious question and an innocent response about the eventual effects of a basic discovery can raise the hopes of the patient far beyond what the scientist had intended.

Press conferences can get out of control. A classic example of this occurred at Dartmouth-Hitchcock Medical Center in Hanover, New Hampshire, on October 16, 1984, when researchers met the press to discuss their work in treating Alzheimer's patients. They had just published an article in the journal *Neurosurgery* on four patients who had been treated with an implantable pump that delivered drugs at a steady rate for extended periods of time. The article included the researchers' subjective impressions that several patients seemed to show improvement. The scientists emphasized that there was no objective data to gauge that improvement however; it was their *impression!*

The Dartmouth PR office called a news conference to have the researchers explain the findings. Charles Petit of the *San Francisco Chronicle* described the event in the February 1985 issue of the *Newsletter of the National Association of Science Writers*, "Dartmouth's Big Story: How It Got Pumped Up and Then Deflated." Although the researchers had intended for the press conference to downplay their work, just the opposite occurred. It resulted in massive coverage—on all three major television networks and in hundreds of newspapers nationwide. More than 2,600 persons seeking treatment contacted Dartmouth in the wake of the news barrage. Victor Cohn, veteran medical correspondent for the *Washington Post*, was quoted as saying, "The story showed complete irresponsibility on the part of the press in handling statistics. Just four patients? Subjective impressions of improvement? Come on here."[11]

### The Patient's Tearful Testimonial

Reporters often turn to patients for medical information.

Patient testimonials offer spicy quotes, delivered in easy-to-understand layman's language, and give a tone of humanness to otherwise dry medicalese. Some patients and their families may solicit press coverage in order to raise money or give publicity to a rare illness in hopes of generating more money and interest in research.

The danger of quoting patients occurs when they are allowed to evaluate the effects of their therapy. What the patient believes to be an effective medication may actually be the placebo effect coming into play. Also, a patient is at a great disadvantage when dealing with the press. Very few have had any experience with reporters. And what the patient/family hopes to gain from press coverage is usually not the same as that which the reporter is striving for. While reporters want personal details that help tell a story vividly, families and patients may wish to guard their privacy.

Problems may arise when a patient decides to withdraw from the public arena. This happens for a variety of reasons: a physician may warn the patient to stop dealing with reporters; the patient's disease may make personal communication impossible. Dr. William DeVries, the first surgeon to successfuly implant a permanent artificial heart in a human being, endured the wrath of many reporters after he began withholding details about his patients.


## Time Restraints: How Packaging Affects the Product

News stories about medicine, or any other subject, are made, not born. Their creators are fallible human beings who face tremendous pressures of time and make mistakes be cause they often must deal with complex information and difficult or uncooperative sources. Although medical stories may sprout from a variety of sources, the process of preparing and packaging the story is much the same. For a morning newspaper, it may happen in the following manner:

Reporter John Jones arrives in the newsroom of the *Daily News* at 10:00 A.M., expecting to put in a full day of work on an in-depth feature story on cancer that he is preparing for the Sunday newspaper. But within a few moments after arriving at his desk, an editor (a news editor or city editor, depending on the size of the newspaper) hands Jones a news release announcing a news conference for noon of that day at Metropolitan Hospital. The news release is cryptic, stating only the time, place and general subject matter—cancer—of the news event. Although no definite decision about using the story is made at this time, the editor places the assignment on the "news budget" for the day, and awaits word from reporter Jones who will call the office immediately following the news briefing.

The news conference draws representatives from all of the major local media, who anxiously await the "major announcement," as the press release had promised. After all, it must be important because doctors are not generally prone to calling news conferences. The conference is delayed for a few moments to allow the TV crews to set up lights.

The doctors are introduced by a hospital public relations person. One of the physicians reads a prepared statement, phrased in complex medical jargon that basically says Metropolitan Hospital will begin testing a new "chemotherapeutic agent" against cancer. He explains the methods of the study, procedures for enrollment of patients, and talks about some of the preliminary findings when the drug was used in "animal models." In closing, the doctors reemphasize the need for "study subjects."

The news conference is opened for questions. Reporter Jones, who has covered the medical beat for three years, asks the doctors to compare the effectiveness of this anti-cancer drug with other drugs used in the past. Another reporter inquires about side effects. A radio reporter, who stopped by the news conference on the way to his regular assignment at city hall, requests the doctors to summarize the study in a few sentences not to exceed 90 seconds—the time alloted during the hourly radio news program.

By 1:00 P.M., the news conference is over, but reporter Jones's work is just beginning. He calls his editor to report what has transpired at the news briefing. "I'm not convinced this is a big story; it sounds more like the hospital is making an appeal for patients," Jones says. The editor asks: "Were the TV and radio guys there?" Jones expresses his concern that the one television crew, which found a patient who plans to participate in the story, would "give the story good play" on the evening telecast. "Then we'll have to have something in tomorrow's paper," the editor says. "We need your story by six."

Reporter Jones hurries back to the newsroom. It's two o'clock; he has four hours to compose a 750-word article, based on the news conference. He first checks his own files for information on the new drug, then he calls the newspaper library ("the morgue"), which keeps articles on particular topics. Neither search turns up much, except a three-year-old news release about another cancer drug study at Metropolitan Hospital. Reporter Jones's only source material must come from the notes he scribbled during the one-hour-long news conference. In deciphering his shorthand, Jones finds that he missed some statistics on recovery rates. He places a call to one of the physicians. "I'm sorry," a polite voice tells the reporter, "but the doctor is in clinic and won't be back until late this afternoon." Jones requests a call-back.

But Jones cannot wait until then to start writing his story, so he contacts another physician in town who has been a good medical source in the past. This doctor, however, is not familiar with the new drug and must reserve comment.

Minutes speed by. There's no time to visit the local medical school library to do a literature search. Jones must begin to compose his story. He has less than two hours before deadline. At 4:30, the editor wants to know some details about the story so the newspaper's layout editors can begin planning the presentation of the news. "Is it Page One?" the editor asks. "No, there are no results in humans. Until now, they've only studied animals," Jones responds. The editor counters, "But a lot of people will be interested, and it's not often that we have doctors holding a news conference, so I think we should give it a good ride."

Jones's story opens like this:

Doctors at Metropolitan Hospital yesterday unveiled plans to study a new anti-cancer drug in a controlled study of patients with leukemia. Although doctors say the drug worked successfully in animal models, they cannot predict whether the drug will have any long-term impact on cancer survival in humans.

Jones turns the story into his editor at 5:45 and is told to wait a few minutes before leaving the office so the editor can read the story. The editor frowns. "The story lacks punch; it doesn't have enough impact to go to page one," he tells Jones. A layout editor has already locked in a spot in the lower right-hand corner of the page, right next to another medical story on the start of flu season. "We have a medical package with a color border around both stories," the editor says. "We're going to have to make the story a little stronger."

A rewrite man gets the task, and produces a new "lead" or first paragraph that reads:

For some patients with acute leukemia, a new drug being used at Metropolitan Medical Center may be the answer to their prayers. Local doctors announced yesterday that the drug, which cured laboratory animals of disease, was now available for use in people.

Journalistically, the story may be considered accurate because it includes the qualifier "may" and it is likely that many patients are probably praying for a cure. But it is also true that the drug "may not" work because animals react differently to chemical agents and some surgical procedures. Yet animal studies are often the subject of medical stories in the popular press (See chapter 13, "The Vasectomy Scare"). For example, early studies of interferon in animals were promising, but when applied to people, it was found to be effective in treating only hairy cell leukemia and basal cell skin carcinoma.

# 3

## Quackery, Flackery, and Hype

Medical hype infests the news media. Webster's dictionary defines hype as a way "to promote or publicize extravagantly" for the purpose of deception, sales, or stimulation. This chapter examines how the press has become a pawn in the game of medical hype.

### Quackery Flourishes

Around the turn of the century, medicine was plagued by hucksters who traveled the countryside touting swamp root, hive syrup, Dr. Hobson's pink pain pills, and Pluto water, among other worthless remedies. They occasionally made their appeals directly to consumers—on street corners and in public meeting halls—but more often they reached the public through newspaper advertisements.

Despite quantum advances in medical knowledge, quackery has grown, even flourished, in recent times. The practice has changed in style but not in substance. The comic pitchman selling elixir from a covered wagon has been replaced by shrewd salesmen and marketing strategists who use the news media to peddle their nostrums.

Today, medical quackery is a $10 billion a year scandal, a congressional committee concluded in 1984 after a four-year investigation of fraudulent medical claims. "The reliance on unproven health methods is as old as man, spawned in pain and desperation," reported the House Subcommittee on Health and Long-Term Care. "When pain is intense and prolonged, the temptation 'to try anything' is almost irresistible."[1]

In the course of its investigation, the committee uncovered advertisements for products that claimed curative powers for nearly every ailment known to man with promises to "cure the incurable—herpes and Alzheimer's disease—and restore the unrestorable—like normal sight to the near sighted or hair to the bald man."

What is quackery? Dr. Oliver Wendell Holmes may have described it best when he said, "Probably in many nostrums and in some pseudo-medical treatments of disease or disturbances there is a grain or two of truth, which, however, has been so magnified and lauded for financial gain that nothing but quackery, deceit or insanity is left."[2] In other words, quackery is the promotion for financial gain of medical remedies known to be false or unproven.

The difference between quackery and the premature release of yet unproven medical research has to do with motive. The quack seeks to make a profit at the expense of the pain and suffering of the public regardless of the results of scientific studies. Senior citizens are the primary target because the incidence of chronic and incurable diseases is higher in this population group.

Discerning a quack from a reputable scientist isn't always easy. Writing in the medical journal *Archives of Internal Medicine*, Dr. Stephan Barrett observed: "Most people think the modern health quack is easy to spot. But he isn't. He wears the cloak of science. He talks in 'scientific' terms. He writes with scientific references. And he is introduced on talk shows as the 'scientist ahead of his time.' The very word 'quack' helps his camouflage by making us think of an outlandish character selling snake oil. . . ."[3]

What is the media's role in quackery? The major news outlet for quackery has been the so-called supermarket press, but all-too-often some of the nation's reputable news magazines and newspapers provide medical charlatans with a vehicle to spread the word about their powerless potions. Quackery seeps into both news stories and mail order advertisements.

One of the most extensive studies of mail-order health advertising was conducted by the quackery committee of the Pennsylvania Medical Society in 1977. In a survey of five hundred nationally circulated news magazines, the committee discovered that about one-fourth of them carried ads for mail-order health products, ranging from blemish removers to aphrodisiacs and various kinds of weight reduction gimmicks, according to Dr. Stephan Barrett, a member of that committee.

The Consumer's Union and editors of the popular *Consumer Reports* books and magazines, conducted another survey of mail-order quackery. Among the findings reported in the 1981 book *Health Quackery* were:

• In mid-1977 and early 1978, eighteen national magazines carried full-page ads for a plastic belt that guaranteed to reduce waistlines from two to four inches in only three days or less. The magazines included *Sports Illustrated* and *Esquire*.

• A full-page ad appeared in twelve major metropolitan newspapers in October 1978 that promoted an "incredible crash diet" that burned away more fat in twenty-four hours than if a person ran fourteen miles a day. Among the newspapers carrying the ad were the *Washington Post* and *Los Angeles Times*.

The Consumer's Union concluded: "Many newspapers that pride themselves on the accuracy and reliability of their news coverage print mail-order health ads without checking even the most outrageous claims."[4]

So who is responsible for insuring the veracity of ad

claims? A majority of Americans believe that mail-order health promotion ads are verified by the press or regulated by a government agency, making it unlikely that serious distortions of the truth about the curative powers of a drug will find their way into print. In reality, however, there is no governmental review of ad claims before they appear in the press. Further, enforcement by the Federal Trade Commission (FTC) lags months, sometimes even years, behind the publication of fraudulent health claims.

### Arthritics Easy Prey

An estimated forty million Americans suffer from arthritis, making it the number one chronic crippling disorder in the country. Because there is no cure for arthritis, its sufferers are easy prey for the quack.

Among the quack cures for arthritis that have drawn media attention, according to the congressional report on quackery, were the following:

—Articles appeared in national tabloids in 1978, 1981, and 1983 extolling bee venom as the "New Cure for Arthritis." But bee venom, according to Dr. Gerald Weissman, director of the division of rheumatology at the National Institutes of Health (NIH), is potentially lethal.

—Catalyst Altered Water (CAW), first developed by Willard Water as a cleaning agent in the 1930s, was featured on CBS-TV's "60 Minutes" on November 23, 1980.[5] The broadcast included testimonials from several people in South Dakota, where the water was discovered, who claimed that the water was helpful to them. The news report also suggested that the FDA and other authorities had tried to block its sale twice. An FDA analysis of the product showed that it contained water spiced by castor oil and three kinds of salt. After the FDA inquiry, the manufacturer of CAW was forced to disavow any medicinal claims in its promotion of the water.

## Controls Lacking, So the Public Suffers

Why does quackery thrive? For several reasons:

—In some cases, people may actually improve after ingesting a quack cure, but improvement does not occur because of the mystic remedy. Instead, patients may be reacting to the placebo effect, a scientifically proven psychological phenomenon, or their disease may have gone into remission.

—The government is doing a poor job of policing the problem. According to the 1984 congressional report, neither state nor federal agencies have strong enforcement programs. The chances of catching the perpetrators of quackery are slim and penalties upon conviction are small. In summary, the quack faces little risk in selling hope to desperate people.

To eliminate quackery, the congressional committee called for a multi-faceted effort that required investment of more money into legitimate medical research, stronger enforcement measures by the FDA and FTC, stiffer penalties against quacks, and the creation of a national health information clearinghouse so the public can learn whether a proposed remedy is legitimate.

The news media could do a lot more to curtail quackery. Reporters and newspaper advertising executives should check out any story or ad about a miracle cure with either a government agency or a reputable scientist before allowing the information to go public. Not to do so contributes to the damage of quacks, which is extensive.

The damage wreaked by the purveyors of quack medicine is much more severe than just financial loss. In some cases, the lives of sick people could have been improved by proper medical procedures. There is also the psychological damage. Victims of quackery suffer further despair just when their hopes had begun to soar.

## Health Care Marketing: A Return to Hucksterism?

During the past decade, a new word has entered the health care vernacular. The word is marketing. While marketing has flourished in American business for some time, medical care providers generally shunned the practice, believing that selling humanitarian services was immoral. But the economics of medicine—an overabundance of hospital beds and a glut of physicians—have forced medical people to reconsider the ethical guidelines that once prohibited them from engaging in self-promotion, a more benign form of "health hype." In the old days, hospitals and clinics relied on "referral networks"—a fancy term for word-of-mouth—for patients. But active solicitation for patients has thrown the traditional system into chaos. As a result, medical providers are in a scramble for survival. The contest is being waged in newsprint and through the electronic airwaves.

Robert M. Cunningham, Jr., associate editor of *Hospitals* magazine, observes that marketing has invaded the hospital field "to the point where it is a rare hospital executive who hasn't attended a seminar or conference where a marketing genius of another industry has been spreading the word about this newly revealed answer to the problems and perplexities of hospitals at a time of crisis, or, at any rate, hypothesized crisis."[6]

A hospital's marketing strategy is usually multifaceted and typically includes a two-pronged media campaign: the purchase of paid commercials in television, radio, and newspapers; and, the use of traditional public relations tactics that seek to use the news columns to tell the hospital's story. The objective in both approaches is the same: to promote the health care institution. By adopting techniques honed by other businesses, hospitals hope to achieve the same kind of payoff. And that means more patients.

## Beware of Flackery

In arguing for their place on the marketing team, public relations people suggest ways to "get into print" without advertising. They contend that a news story carries more weight with the viewer or reader because of its supposed "objectivity." The fact that an unbiased reporter prepares the story lends more credibility to the product, the PR line goes.

Newsmen often call public relations people "flacks." The origin of the word, according to Webster's dictionary, is unknown but it is defined as "one who provides publicity, a press agent," and is a variation of "flak"—the bursting of shells fired from antiaircraft guns. News people generally use the term in a derogatory sense because there is an ingrained mistrust between news people who must deal with the PR person whose job it is to publicize, promote, and hype.

"PR people have in them both a little bit of John the Baptist and a Mississippi snake doctor," suggests one cynical newsman. "They are totally dedicated to their Messianic cause, but unfortunately their product is sometimes worthless." PR people bristle at the suggestion that they practice subterfuge in dealing with the press. They defend themselves on grounds that publicity is educational and good for the public's health.

Public relations-generated news should be viewed critically, warns Warren Burkett, a professor of journalism at the University of Texas at Austin. In his textbook *News Reporting: Science, Medicine and High Technology,* Burkett writes:

Media science writers keep in mind that stories prepared by business firms, universities, hospitals, and other institutions are aimed at promoting the welfare of the organizations, not at satisfying the needs of readers or viewers. A hospital may trumpet its purchase of a new piece of medical equipment but neglect to say there are others in town just like it. A hospital or clinic may announce the availability of a new medical procedure without giving background or perspective, such as the risks involved or alternative treatments. Drug companies' publicists are notorious for promoting slight variations on existing drugs ("me too drugs") without mentioning competitors' products. Side effects, those reactions that accompany any drug's intended effects, seldom get mentioned in press releases."[7]

## Physicians Enter the Fray

Physicians also are playing the marketing game to lure patients into their waiting rooms. Since 1979, doctors have been permitted to advertise their services. Some doctors have turned to PR and marketing people for help in finding patients. In a 1983 report, the American Medical Association (AMA) found that 40 percent of physicians have adopted some new marketing techniques within the last two years. "This indicates that a significant proportion of physicians are beginning to adopt measures to cope with a more competitive environment," the report said.[8]

Competition has resulted from a glut of doctors that has far outpaced the nation's population growth. From 1970 to 1980, the number of active physicians nationwide rose from 311,000 to 436,000. By the year 2000, the AMA projects the number will grow to 666,000—an increase of 50 percent over 1980—while the population is expected to rise by only 18 percent.

*Medical World News,* a magazine oriented to the general practitioner, carries a "Marketing Your Practice" column to advise doctors on ways to increase their patient numbers. For example, the December 9, 1985, column, "Take the Initiative to Get Newspaper Coverage," prepared by a Houston marketing firm, said: "A local newspaper article about you and your practice is an excellent means of increasing your patient base. And preparing a press release—either by yourself or with the help of public relations professionals—is a legitimate way for you to obtain such favorable publicity."[9]

## Organizational Appeals Tap Emotions

National organizations that fund research and rehabilitation in a particular disease wage aggressive media campaigns to gain visibility and to spur fund-raising. Many have been in the medical hype game for years; they know how to appeal to the public's emotions. Representatives of these groups provide eager sources for the press. Some organizations even cater to press needs by holding annual "science writer" conferences where "new and significant" developments are made public.

Dr. Franz J. Ingelfinger, the late editor of the *New England Journal of Medicine*, described their zealousness this way: "In their desperate search for funds, national organizations interested in cancer or cardiovascular disease bombarded the public with public-relations maneuvers that rival the promotion of cereals and dog foods that offer, in my opinion, the misleading implication that if only enough money were made available, dread diseases would be eliminated pronto."[10]

While many of these organizations are respected, some lesser known foundations spend a very small percentage of the donated funds on medical research. The public should be cautious when it comes to supporting medical research when the pitch is purely emotional.

## The Medical Evangelist

Another form of "medical hype" unrelated to filling hospital beds or bolstering a doctor's patient census is self-promotion of medical research by the medical evangelist. This individual isn't motivated as much by monetary incentive as the need to share the "good news" with colleagues and the world.

Physician-author William Nolen calls these individuals "medical zealots." Just prior to his death in December 1986, Nolen published an article by that title in the *American Scholar* magazine in which he revealed numerous cases of how "accepted" medical ideas and techniques had changed through the years, even though their initial unveilings were hailed by key medical people as "breakthroughs." Because of the fallability and inexactitude of medical science, he warned that the public beware of medical evangelists. Nolen wrote:

These doctors are absolutely convinced that they know the best rules for the human race to live by, from the physical point of view. (They are comparable to religious zealots who are certain they know how we should live morally and spiritually.) They don't lie—they don't even intentionally exaggerate—but their enthusiasm sometimes carries them away so that they claim more for their research than the results actually warrant. Because many of them are researchers in the academic world, they are eager to publish their results and, if possible, to be the first to do so.[11]

Even the best medical journals can't catch every inaccuracy. For example, Nolen told the story of how a prominent surgical journal once carried a regular "reappraisal" column in which a reviewer would reassess an article about a medical breakthrough from a year or two previously. "Often this reappraisal would amount to a negation of the previous article," Nolen said.

## The Future: Health Hype Overload

We are likely to hear, read, and see more health promotion

in years to come from the health care industry that seeks to get its message to the consumer in a positive light. Hospitals are expected to face even stronger competition from alternative facilities, such as hospices, birthing centers, and health maintenance organizations, according to a 1984 study by the American College of Hospital Administrators. As one official says: "We must compete to survive."

The intrusion of marketing into the medical arena means consumers must be ever cautious when responding to health messages. Ask yourself, what is the intention of the party pushing the information? Is the hospital seeking to fill a new ward, to pay off the purchase of an expensive piece of technology, or to actually improve the health of the community?

Remember, it's the PR person's job to promote—read that sell—the product. That goal is achieved by emphasizing the positive, and either ignoring or downplaying the negative. The press release on a new drug is not going to begin with a statement of side effects. PR people are often caught in a vice between their employers and the media. With the possible exception of a few "information offices" at some universities, few PR people are able to speak frankly about the merits of a medical discovery at their institution.

The problem with all of this ballyhooing is that people who are sick or dying don't have the tools to evaluate the value of medical services. Medical promotion differs radically from other forms of advertising. As Dr. Dana Johnson of the University of Minnesota states: "It's different from trying different handsoap or hamburgers; you can lose your life in the process of 'testing' out a hospital or physician."[12]

# II  Raising Hopes, Dashing Dreams, Spreading Fear

Snake Venom Offers Hope for Multiple Sclerosis Patients . . . Acupuncture Restores Hearing to the Deaf . . . Laetrile Cures Cancer . . . Vasectomies Linked to Heart Disease. Impressionable news consumers have been led astray by splashy headlines such as these. This section examines fifteen news stories that dealt with medical breakthroughs and public health issues.

# 4 Snake Venom and Multiple Sclerosis

For centuries mankind has been fascinated by the notion that venom from poisonous snakes might hold curative powers. Even today, the snake remains a symbol for many health organizations despite the fact that the healing ability of snake venom has not passed scientific scrutiny.

In 1979, two major American news organizations—CBS-TV's "60 Minutes" and the weekly news magazine *Newsweek*—and numerous smaller newspapers and television stations gave unwarranted credibility to the use of snake venom as a cure for multiple sclerosis and arthritis. The stories described the work of snake handler William Haast and Miami pediatrician Dr. Ben Sheppard, who were using cobra and krait venom to treat patients. The publicity spurred thousands of sufferers to flock to a Miami, Florida, clinic to receive a potentially lethal venom-filled drug known as PROven, which had not received FDA approval.

## MS: A Chronic, Degenerative Disease

Multiple sclerosis, or "MS," is a relatively common disease of the nervous system, characterized by premature death of nerve cells. MS is both chronic and degenerative: once the slow process of deterioration begins, it cannot be deterred. There is not a single case of recovery, although many patients experience periods of remission. Indeed, in some cases the disease is severe for a few months to a year and then is completely inactive for a decade or more.

Onset of symptoms usually occurs in the twenties and thirties, starting with muscle problems such as clumsiness, a sense of heaviness, and a tendency to drop things. The initial symptom may be something as simple as a tingling or brief loss of sensation. The first attack may last a few days or a few weeks, and then clear up. The progression of symptoms is so unpredictable that any experimental therapy must be tested very carefully to be sure that the treatment is really making the difference, because the patient could be in temporary remission.[1]

Although the exact cause of MS is unknown, scientists generally believe that it results from damage to myelin—the insulation that surrounds nerve fibers located in the brain and spinal cord. Nerves cannot work normally when myelin is under attack. The disease worsens as more patches of myelin are damaged.

Few diseases in the world are being studied more intensely than MS. In 1979, more than 360 research articles about MS appeared in the medical literature. The major research effort devoted to MS can be attributed to its high incidence; MS strikes between fifty to one hundred of every one hundred thousand adults in temperate climates or an estimated five hundred thousand Americans.

### Venom Use Excites News Media

PROven was the reported brainchild of William Haast, owner and director of the Miami Serpentarium, a major South Florida tourist attraction. Haast began producing snake venom for research in 1948, first using it in an attempt to counter the effects of the polio virus, then later experimenting on MS and arthritis. According to news accounts, Haast gave some of the venom to the late Dr. Sheppard, a Miami pediatrician, who used it on himself for rheumatoid arthritis.

Believing that the venom relieved his pain, Sheppard begin in early 1978 to administer venom to his patients who suffered from a variety of diseases.[2]

Initially, only a few patients received venom. But Sheppard's waiting room began to swarm with clients after word about the unorthodox treatment spread across the continent via the news media. The first news report about venom-treatment surfaced under rather strange circumstances. The Miami press had learned that a shipment of one thousand krait snakes from China had been lost en route to Miami. That was a story in itself, but when a local TV station discovered what the poisonous snakes were intended for, the snake story mushroomed. In February 1979, the story was featured in *SKY*, a Delta Airlines in-flight magazine. The *SKY* article brought Sheppard to the attention of the FDA, which began investigating PROven in the spring of 1979—and other news media.

The unorthodox clinic gained national exposure on December 16, 1979, when CBS-TV's "60 Minutes" devoted a thirteen-minute segment to snake venom treatment. The story was an eye-catcher; it opened with a cobra being milked of its deadly venom. The story was controversial; it suggested scientists were foot-dragging in their studies of snake-venom treatment.

Not one of the 360 research articles published in 1979 dealt with snake-venom therapy, according to a survey of that year in *Index Medicus*, a listing of articles carried in legitimate peer-reviewed medical and scientific journals. Yet many scientists reported major advances in rehabilitation and treatment of symptoms such as the loss of bladder function.

Despite the scientific community's efforts to dissuade "60 Minutes" from airing the story, CBS-TV informed an estimated sixty-five million Americans that the government and National Multiple Sclerosis Society were reluctant to investigate a potentially effective treatment. Dr. Byron Waksman, head of the research group of the MS society, charged that CBS was guilty of "straight media pressure" rather than attempting to deal with the issue objectively.[3]

## Docs Fail to Thwart Media Blitz

In November 1979, on the eve of the "60 Minutes" broadcast, the FDA convened a special workshop to discuss the effect of snake venom on both MS and arthritis. The agency apparently hoped that strong statements from experts would turn the press away from the story. Both Sheppard and Haast testified at the hearing. When questioned by FDA investigators, Dr. Sheppard acknowledged that his patients' diagnoses were not always confirmed in his clinic, and that he had not made a systematic or objective measure of their response to venom treatment. He acknowledged that he had not routinely examined patients.[4]

Nevertheless, Sheppard based his support of snake venom treatment on his patients' personal stories—about 63 percent of those with MS responded to initial treatments, and 20 percent showed lasting improvement, primarily bladder incontinence, he claimed. Sheppard offered the FDA panel no medical records to substantiate his claims nor had he submitted his work for critical review in peer-reviewed scientific journal.

At the end of the workshop, neurologists and rheumatologists concluded that Sheppard's experience didn't show PROven was effective in treating MS. The pediatrician's impressions of patient improvement were just what could be expected from spontaneous remissions or the result of a placebo effect, the FDA stated.

While the FDA and Multiple Sclerosis Society were lobbying CBS to pull its snake venom story, *Newsweek* pulled a news scoop with a December 3 story titled, "Snake Oil or Medicine?" In the article, four patients were quoted, all claiming that snake venom had relieved their suffering. "It's a miracle," one patient was quoted as saying. Another remarked: "Now I can walk well. I can even go disco dancing."

News coverage spurred thousands of MS patients to head to Miami seeking snake venom treatment for multiple sclerosis, arthritis, and amyotrophic lateral sclerosis (popularly known as Lou Gehrig's disease). It also prompted two research efforts to determine the true value of venom. *Science* magazine commented: "The publicity has brought to a head pressure on the Food and Drug Administration to sponsor clinical trials for the drug, even though there is no hard evidence that is efficacious and definite scientific reason to suppose it should be."[5]

Press attention also forced the National Multiple Sclerosis Society to become involved in the controversy. The MS Society arranged to conduct clinical studies of venom; it actually had trouble finding reputable scientists to conduct the study because "half the investigators we talked to wouldn't touch it with a 10-foot pole," said Dr. Waksman. Why the reluctance to perform the research? Because scientists already knew the snake handlers' claims were unfounded, based on known medical facts. Haast contended that nerve-growth factor (NGF) was the rationale for snake venom to heal MS patients. However, NGF is not found in cobra or krait venoms, only in viper venom. Besides, neurologists pointed out, even if NGF were present in cobra and krait venom, the factor's primary effect is on the sympathetic nervous system, whereas MS is a disease of the white matter. MS affects the cells that produce myelin, the connective tissue between neurons, while NGF acts on the neurons directly.

Finally, researchers at the University of Chicago and the University of Arizona agreed to conduct placebo-controlled, double-blind studies of cobra venom under strict laboratory guidelines. Hundreds of thousands of people awaited the answers. But the studies were never conducted, Waksman said, because the researchers never received the venom from the serpentarium. Meanwhile, a separate group of researchers independently testing venom for another neurological disorder, amyotrophic lateral sclerosis, reported in the *Archives of Neurology,* that venom "lacked clinical effectiveness."[6] Based on its findings, the FDA announced that venom was an absolutely worthless therapy, and could even be dangerous to patients. According to the FDA, a young Texas woman died while being treated with the venom.

Dr. Richard T. Johnson, professor of neurology at Johns Hopkins University and a well-known MS expert, discussed the impact of snake venom publicity at the 1981 meeting of the Council for the Advancement and Support of Education. He said:

> Many people say it makes no difference if some quack cure is publicized; it's new and makes good copy. The fact is that millions of dollars are spent on unproven or even dangerous therapies. Such reports often divert the patient from seeking proper treatment for the disease. And more important, looking at it from the vantage point of a neurologist who takes care of patients with chronic diseases and limited life expectancies, publishing dubious cures takes time away from patients' lives. Life is finite for all of us, and if a patient has two or three years left, spending six months of that time chasing quack cures is tragic. This fault, I think, often lies with the media.[7]

### A Triple Tragedy

The tragedy of the "60 Minutes" exposé and coverage by other news media is three-fold. First, media attention led thousands of patients and their families to doubt their doctors and put unrealistic hopes in a risky procedure. Second, the ensuing controversy diverted scientists' time and valuable research funds from constructive studies to useless studies that only served to formally disprove an already dubious remedy. Finally, journalists missed an opportunity to run a story that might have truly improved the lives of MS patients. Among the 360 articles published in 1979, several dealt with rehabilitation and the problems that MS patients have in finding employment. Imagine the impact of a "60 Minutes" story that focused on job discrimination against MS employees!

By conventional journalistic standards, the *Newsweek* article could be considered fair because it was balanced. Besides statements by patients, the story included comments from a physician who argued that "there is not a shred of persuasive evidence that it [venom] is of any value." However, suffering patients don't have time to weigh such arguments, and many are likely to believe the testimonials of "cured" individuals like themselves.

But what about the patients who reported benefit from cobra venom? How do we explain their miraculous recovery? One must remember that MS follows a *variable course*. Many patients experience spontaneous remissions that can last weeks, months, or years. Medical science does not completely understand the body's nervous system. Another factor in patient's improvement is their psychological and emotional state. Strong-willed individuals often do better in fighting off illness.

Dr. Robert J. Slater, director of medical programs of the National Multiple Sclerosis Society, noted in an article in the *American Journal of Nursing* that 70 percent of MS patients will show improvement at some time during the illness, regardless of what is done. "If a new treatment is used at a time of improvement, 70 percent of patients and their physicians will be convinced the treatment was responsible, forgetting that the improvement might have occurred without treatment," he wrote.[8]

Sheppard died in March 1980 but Haast continued to sell PROven until March 1982 when the U.S. District Court for the Southern District of Florida permanently enjoined him from making and distributing the drug.[9]

# 5 A Dangerous Cure for Cystic Acne

Between 1979 and 1983, the public was deluged with media coverage of a new drug for the treatment of severe cystic acne, a sometimes disfiguring skin disease that affects thousands of Americans. Unlike pimply acne common among teenagers, cystic acne causes deep red carbuncle-like sores that remain for years and leave permanent pits and scars. The psychological effects of the condition can be devastating as well.

The anti-acne drug, marketed under the name Accutane and manufactured by Hoffman-La Roche Inc. received FDA approval on May 22, 1982, after six years of tests at ten U.S. medical centers. Approximately 90 percent of treatment-resistant patients receiving Accutane showed significant improvement.

The media began touting the drug's "curative" powers as early as 1979, when preliminary clinical data began to appear in medical journals. The tempo of coverage picked up as FDA action neared, and reached a peak once it became available to patients. Most press reports were upbeat—quoting patients and physicians who praised the drug's phenomenal healing power—and either ignored or downplayed the drug's potential for causing birth defects.

By 1985, Accutane use had been associated with more than 30 babies born with deformities that included blindness, deafness, cleft palates, heart defects, and craniofacial distortions. At least 100 fetuses were aborted by women who were taking the drug, according to one medical study.

"Relying, by and large, on drug company and FDA evaluation of the product, reporters had played up the drug's benefits and minimized its hazards. By failing to adequately warn girls and women of childbearing age of the danger, the news media unwittingly shared responsibility for the casualties," wrote Jim Sibbison, an AP reporter for fifteen years and a former press officer of the FDA, in an in-depth *Columbia Journalism Review* article on press coverage of the drug industry.[1]

### Pimples, Pits, and Pilosebaceous Follicles

Probably no disease causes more frustration among teenagers than acne. But the problem becomes severe in only a small number. While 80 percent of adolescents and young adults will have at least one bout with acne, only 2 percent of them suffer the severe form of the disease known as cystic acne. Besides their unsightly appearance, patients suffer terrible pain because the lesions are tender and bleed easily.

The basic problem of cystic acne starts in small skin structures called "pilosebaceous follicles" that are found in large numbers on the face, back, and chest. Each follicle consists of a tiny but active sebaceous gland, which secretes a substance called sebum, connected with a hair remnant and narrow channel leading to the skin surface. Acne occurs when those channels either leak or become plugged with sebum, causing the follicles to expand into visible lumps known as comedones. If a comedo stays closed at the skin surface, it becomes what is commonly called a "whitehead." If it opens, exposed pigment causes the comedo to become a "blackhead," a discoloration that is not caused by dirt, which is a common myth. Disfiguring cysts and abscesses can form if excessive pressure within the comedones produces leaking into surrounding skin.[2]

## Media Heralds Drug's Debut

Accutane's media debut came on the evening of February 14, 1979, when CBS-TV and NBC-TV aired stories based on information in the next day's issue of the *New England Journal of Medicine*, the same issue cited earlier. The *Journal* carried the results of a study by Dr. Gary L. Peck and other scientists at the National Cancer Institute (NCI) who used 13-*cis*-retinoic acid (the drug's chemical name) on fourteen patients with severe treatment-resistant cystic acne. They claimed that thirteen patients "experienced complete clearing of their disease; the other had 75 percent improvement."[3]

On the next day, newspapers throughout the nation carried lengthy articles distributed by the nation's two major news services—United Press Internaional (UPI) and the AP. But of these major media outlets, reaching the vast majority of news-consuming Americans, only the NBC-TV story by reporter Jessica Savitch mentioned that the drug had the potential to cause birth defects!

ABC-TV aired its first story on Accutane use on November 9, 1981. Reporter George Strait's four-minute "special assignment" segment included pro-drug comments from Dr. James Leyden, a clinical investigator working for Hoffman-La Roche, and from three test subjects who praised the drug's healing powers. "I now look forward to a normal life" thanks to Accutane, said one young man. The drug's potentially harmful side effects were not mentioned in the story.

On the eve of FDA action, the media picked up the story again. UPI issued a story to its subscribers on May 8, 1982, quoting a physician as saying that it would be "almost immoral" for the FDA to deny drug approval of a drug "so effective for a disease that is so crushing." The UPI story mentioned chapped lips as one of the drug's principal side effects.

The AP, which covered the Accutane story more extensively than any other media organization, issued dispatches to its subscribers during the clinical trials, upon FDA approval, and when it became available in pharmacies. The tone of those stories was typically upbeat. Here's how the news service described the FDA approval on May 21, 1982:

The government approved today a new prescription drug for the treatment of the most disfiguring form of acne.

The product, 13-*cis*-retinoic acid, has been shown to cause long-term remission of cystic acne in test patients. It is a derivative of Vitamin A and has the chemical name isotretinoin.

The drug will be sold by Hoffman-La Roche of Nutley, N.J., under the name Accutane. The U.S. is the first nation to approve the product.

About 300,000 Americans suffer from cystic acne. It is a chronic disorder of the oil glands primarily of the face, neck and back. In most cases, it produces deep pitting and scarring.

The most common side effect of the new drug is severe drying and chapping of lips. In some of the patients, it has been associated with elevation of blood serum triglycerides or of cholesterol levels.

The FDA, in approving the product, reminded physicians that less powerful preparations are available for common acne.[4]

Absent from the great majority of media reports was a mention of the need for extreme caution to avoid using the drug during the period of conception or gestation. The manufacturer knew of the potential of birth defects among children born to mothers who had taken Accutane; that fact was mentioned on page three of a four-page news release given to reporters. The FDA news release said nothing of the risk.

Just how potent is Accutane? According to dermatologists at Duke University, "Few agents are as poisonous to the developing fetus. Extreme caution to avoid use of Accutane during the period of conception or gestation is indicated."[5] The *Harvard Medical School Health Letter* said of the drug, "It is now apparent that Accutane is as capable of producing devastating defects as is thalidomide."[6]

Reporters could easily have uncovered details on risk factors by checking some of the early published reports in the medical literature, or by reading the patient package insert (PPI) that accompanies every prescription drug. The PPI was available to reporters from the FDA, drug manufacturers, or any pharmacist. The PPI warned that animal studies indicated that "teratogenic [causing birth defects] effects may occur." The drug's potency was so great that the FDA gave it a pregnancy rating of X, which means that no woman, either pregnant or considering becoming pregnant, should take the drug.

A close reading of Peck's original report in the *New England Journal of Medicine* also would have tipped reporters off to the drug's potential dangers. Peck and his colleagues warned that, "Fertile women treated with 13-*cis*-RA should take contraceptive precautions during therapy." An editorial by Dr. Peter E. Pochi of University Hospital in Boston, Massachusetts, that accompanied the research article in the medical journal, also pointed to the danger: "Particularly important . . . is the known teratogenicity of the retinoid class of drugs."[7] The news media, with the exception of NBC, missed that critical caveat.

Fearing that the public would misread the barrage of press coverage, the *Harvard Medical School Health Letter,* which aims its editorial content at a general readership and is easily accessible to medical reporters, cautioned in its May 1979 issue:

. . . recently, the media featured the success story of a "new" pill for acne which produced dramatic results in 14 severe and resistant cases—as reported in the New England Journal of Medicine. However, the promise of this medication . . . has been known for several years within dermatology circles and its potential value is new only to the media and the general public. It is expected that several more years of testing for safety will be necessary before release for general use. Even then, many observers expect that it will be used only for the relatively small number of acne patients who do not respond to the (other) treatment measures . . . *It is also expected that this pill may not be generally available to women because it is likely to cause birth defects.*[8]

The doctors and editors at Harvard were worried about another public health hazard created by the media's coverage of Accutane. They warned that because of all the publicity associated with vitamin A treatment of acne, many patients might turn to self-medication with excessive amounts of natural vitamin A pills. Such a practice could lead to serious side effects, including liver damage, the physician newsletter warned.

Concerned about the avalanche of pro-drug publicity and possible misinterpretation of the drug's intended use, Hoffman-La Roche sent an urgent letter to doctors in the fall of 1982 to warn them about the possibly harmful side effects. The warning letter began in capital letters: "BECAUSE TERATOGENICITY HAS BEEN OBSERVED IN ANIMALS, PREGNANT PATIENTS OR THOSE WHO INTEND TO BECOME PREGNANT SHOULD NOT RECEIVE ACCUTANE."

## Deformed Babies Linked to Drug Use

One of the first public reports linking the drug to deformed babies surfaced in the *New York Times* on July 26, 1983.[9] The article told of three women who had given birth to deformed babies. In September, the Health Research Group of Washington, D.C., charged that Accutane had been oversold by its manufacturer.[10] The day after that charge became public, the FDA convened a special panel to investigate risks associated with Accutane.

Then, on March 26, 1984, the FDA took the unprecedented

action of warning all blood banks not to accept blood from patients undergoing Accutane treatment. At least eighteen deformed babies had been born to mothers who had taken the drug, while another twenty-one pregnant women had elected to have abortions, according to one published report. The drug company notified one hundred thousand physicians of the problem.[11]

Because of the growing number of deformed babies, a group of researchers from government, Hoffman-La Roche, and several medical schools investigated 154 human pregnancies with fetal exposure to the drug. In October 1985, they reported their findings in the *New England Journal of Medicine*. Of the 154 exposures, there were ninety-five elective abortions and twelve spontaneous abortions. Twenty-six children were born without major malformations, but twenty-one were born with major malformations. The article also reported that an estimated 160 women of childbearing age had taken the drug since it was first introduced. The researchers concluded: "Our data suggest that many of the exposurers during pregnancy were potentially preventable. We found that 67 percent of the exposed pregnancies were among women who were either pregnant when therapy began or were not using contraception while taking isotretinoin. These exposures could have been prevented if the guidelines for the treatment in women had been followed."[12]

Unlike the drug's debut, the follow-up research was ignored by most of the popular media that had actively promoted the drug a few years earlier, although the public health message contained in the report certainly had major public impact.

## A Problem of Semantics

Almost all drugs have potentially harmful side effects, but

side effects may be downplayed or ignored in news coverage because they get in the way of the central message, which is the forward thrust of science that gives hope to suffering people. Qualifiers tend to make a story more complicated, and these details may be lost in the editing process as the story is groomed to fit a finite space.

Medical news consumers should be wary of any new drug that makes its debut in a "news conference" format. When you ask your physician for a "new" medication, ask what side effects surfaced in animal studies and clinical studies in humans. News media reports may either carry only passing reference to side effects, or fail to mention them at all.

The Accutane story points out several failings of medical reporting. First, it illustrates the semantic problem inherrent in popular news writing. Because headlines are made to fit space, rather than subject, copyeditors shortened the story to "acne" rather than "cystic acne," thus leaving the impression that an all-purpose acne medication was available. A casual listener or reader may have interpreted the news announcements as saying there was a cure for common adolescent acne that affects millions. Headlines failed to differentiate between the two forms of acne. For example, *Newsweek's*, September 13, 1982, aricle was titled, "Now, A Real Cure for Acne."

Second, the Accutane story shows that medical reporting by general publications tends to be superficial. Reporters lack either the time or expertise to dig out other facts from medical journal articles. They may simply not know the right questions to ask.

Some physicians also were misled by the hoopla surrounding Accutane's market debut, and incorrectly prescribed the drug for less severe acne. According to Dr. Ronald C. Hansen, writing in *Arizona Medicine*, "It is evident that enthusiasm for the new 'cure' for acne has caused physicians to prescribe isotretinoin for nonscarring and noncystic acne, and for acne in which conventional therapy has not been optimized. This practice is not consistent with the intent of the manufacturers of isotretinoin, and may not be in the long-term best interest of the patients."[13]

Who's to blame for the media hype of Accutane? Responsibility must be shared. Medical reporters failed to dig into the story beyond the superficial press release, while physicians were too quick to applaud the drug before they had thoroughly evaluated the scientific data.

# 6 The Sulindac Seduction

On November 1, 1978, newspapers throughout America were saturated with a remarkable medical news story—the discovery of what was reported to be a new non-steroidal, anti-inflammatory drug to treat arthritis, a painfully chronic ailment that plagues more than twenty-five million Americans. The media blitz surprised the medical community, raised the hopes of many elderly and desperate people, and prompted a debate on "what's medical news?" in a prestigious medical journal. Doctors criticized the sensational nature of the press reports; reporters claimed they were only doing their jobs.

## News Release Whets Press Appetite

It all began with a simple news release, issued by the public relations office of Merck Sharp & Dohme Pharmaceutical Company, inventors of sulindac (marketed under the name Clinoril). Dissemination of the news release was supposed to coincide with the FDA's approval of sulindac for use in the United States; the drug was already available in Europe. The FDA planned no major news event to herald the new drug.

The Merck news release read, in part: "Relief from the pain and disabling joint symptoms of five major arthritic diseases is now possible with a single anti-inflammatory drug that has been found to be even better tolerated than aspirin." Later, the news release quoted Dr. Lewis H. Sarett, Merck's senior vice president for science technology, who called the company's drug "a major advance" that would bring benefit to a "much broader range of patients." The rest of the news release followed the same vein of hopeful optimism.

The sulindac news release resulted in stories that were featured prominently in newspapers throughout the country, especially in media markets with large elderly populations. Both major wire services, the AP and UPI, distributed stories to their subscribers, thus reaching nearly every radio and television station in the country, and practically all 1,750 daily newspapers. Some press reports and headlines embellished the claims of the drug company announcement, but that was understandable because of the upbeat nature of the news release, a common tool of public relations people and publicists to generate media interest in a product, person, or event.

Here's how the wire service stories began:

ASSOCIATED PRESS—A new drug went on the market today that may allow arthritis sufferers to put away their aspirin bottles and find new pain relief with fewer side effects.

The drug is sulindac and its developers tout it as a substitute for aspirin, the drug most widely used against arthritis.

UNITED PRESS INTERNATIONAL—One dose of a new drug for major arthritis ills that affect 30 million Americans packs the anti-inflammatory power of up to eight aspirin—but with fewer side effects, scientists reported yesterday.

## A Vulnerable Audience

There is a massive public interest in arthritis. According to the National Arthritis Foundation, arthritis sufferers are "the most exploited of all victims of diseases in the country today" and they spend an estimated $485 million a year on worthless remedies, treatments, devices, and gimmicks. This population of chronically afflicted people is particularly sensitive to the latest medical breakthrough reported by the mass media.

How did arthritis sufferers respond to the sulindac announcement? The experience of the retirement community of Sun City, Arizona, population fifty thousand, may be typical of how other elderly people reacted throughout the country. Upon reading the news reports, patients contacted their physicians; some demanded the new drug while others threatened to stop taking their current medications. Dr. Alan H. Wallace, an arthritis specialist in the area, said many of his patients were desperate to try the new medication. His office was inundated with telephone calls. Some patients without appointments even stopped in to get the new drug, which they believed would finally bring permanent relief from pain.

So distressed by the exaggerated claims about sulindac, Wallace attacked press coverage in a letter to the *New England Journal of Medicine.*

Without exception, the physicians in this metropolitan area received numerous telephone calls on November 1, when the mass media released information on the new "wonder drug" sulindac. To aggravate the situation a bit more, our early experience with the drug has been nowhere as great as predicted in these promotions. It is of interest that this unfortunate publicity has somewhat dwarfed a recent FDA ruling in which the drug penicillamine was approved as an agent to induce remission of rheumatoid disease.[1]

Two physicians at Stanford University Medical Center in California, Drs. Cody Wasner and Brian Kotzin, used even stronger language in their characterization of press coverage.

We find the sulindac news release deplorable. Imagine a similar promotion practice for each cancer chemotherapeutic agent that is newly released by the FDA! Although official pharmaceutical quotations regarding the drug were carefully worded to stay within the known data, the effect was misleading. It is difficult to separate the contribution of the media from that of the pharmaceutical company;

however, we believe that the company has a responsibility not to allow this type of deception.[2]

In another letter, three private physicians wrote: "One can't blame them (patients) for inundating their physicians with requests for the 'new wonder drug,' for they want the latest available therapy."[3]

The outcry from arthritis sufferers was so great that both the drug manufacturer and the Arthritis Foundation of America issued statements designed to downplay the media hoopla and soften the expectations of patients. After receiving hundreds of phone calls in a few days after the announcement, a Merck public relations manager was quoted as saying: "We think it would be very unfortunate if patients considered this innovation to be a cure because, as we said in the original announcement, advances against arthritis do not come as miracles." The AP story carrying this statement also pointed out that Merck stock rose 5.25 points on the New York Stock Exchange on the day of the original sulindac announcement.[4]

In a two-page analysis of the drug, the Arthritis Foundation observed that benefits of sulindac seemed to be about equal to phenylbutazone, another drug that was introduced without the media fanfare and promotion efforts of the manufacturer. Seeking to put the new drug in context, the foundation suggested that sulindac, like other non-steroidal anti-inflammatory drugs, would play a role in the treatment of rheumatic diseases. But patients should allow their own doctor to determine which drug or treatment is appropriate for a particular patient, the foundation added.

In defense of the news release, its author Alton Blakeslee, claimed that the Arthritis Foundation was informed before the press announcement. Difficulties in Merck's mailing advance notices of the drug's availability to physicians meant that many doctors first learned of the drug in newspaper stories. Advertisements didn't begin to appear in medical journals until November 3—two days after doctors learned of the drug's approval in the mass media.

After several weeks of letters in the *New England Journal of Medicine* that attacked Merck and the press, Blakeslee wrote to defend his work. He stated:

> One detects, in the complaints, a tinge of Olympian outrage over embarrassment that patients knew something (about a new drug) that physicians didn't! Zounds! How simple to reply to responsible, interested patients: "Oh? I haven't heard of that yet. But I'll check it out, and find out if it would be useful to you." Patients should be pleased to receive personal interest from an always-busy physician who maintains his cool and professionalism.[5]

In an effort to quell the controversy, Dr. Arnold S. Relman, editor of the *New England Journal of Medicine*, wrote that, in his opinion, the major fault was in the news media "who chose to treat the release as if it heralded an important new medical discovery." He noted that sulindac was just one in a line of many non-steroidal anti-inflammatory drugs that had been developed during the past decade. Relman also pointed out that, based on the medical literature, sulindac "is about as effective as aspirin or phenylbutazone, although possibly a little better tolerated."[6]

### Beware of Market Debuts

Relman hoped medical reporters would learn from the experience. He commented that savvy medical reporters should know the difference between "a bona fide medical advance and the market debut of a new pharmaceutical product. One is usually reported in a reputable medical journal. The other is commerce."

Gullible reporters, always looking for a good story, often

fail to thoroughly research the subject. In this case, if they had taken more time—and time, of course, is precious in the news business—they would have learned from other researchers that the drug was not the cure-all that it seemed. Craftily worded news releases, especially when they include sparkling quotes and grandiose promises, are sure bait to catch a hungry reporter.

Defenders of the news media might argue that the sulindac miscue was an exceptional case. Perhaps the regular medical reporter was on vacation, and his fill-in didn't have the medical sources to contact for another more critical view of the drug. Also, doctors were caught unprepared because of the snafu in the Merck mail room. But the story still illustrates the lack of safeguards in the media. There's no guarantee that the claims of one scientist or medical manufacturer will be countered by appropriate critics. UPI quoted Merck's own scientist directly from the news release. AP quoted a researcher who received grant support by Merck. Neither story contained comments from individuals who could be considered "objective" arthritis experts, without ties to the manufacturer.

There's another lesson in the "sulindac seduction" that serves as a warning to medical news consumers. The public should be wary of all announcements in the popular press in which company spokesmen are quoted, medical products touted, or breakthroughs claimed. You may not be getting the whole story. Don't fall prey; your health depends on it.

# 7 An "Apocryphal" Tale About Cerebral Palsy

One of the oldest and most popular running events in Atlanta is the annual Peachtree 10K Road Race, held every July 4. Thousands of runners flock to the Georgia city to participate in the race, which draws extensive news media attention. Year in and year out, press coverage is the same: pictures of the throng of runners at the starting line, interviews with the winners, and special feature articles about exceptional athletes.

## Arnold—A Special Athlete

In the aftermath of the 1979 race, the *Atlanta Constitution* carried a story about one of those "special athletes." His name was Arnold, a teenager with cerebral palsy who ran and finished the race in ninety minutes. The July 7 article ("The Race Is Not to the Swift, Nor the Battle to Strong") by health and science writer Roger Witherspoon vividly described Arnold's excruciating ordeal in training and then his heroic struggle to finish the 6.2 mile course. Witherspoon wrote:

> In the beginning he (Arnold) could never make it for more than a half mile without falling—he just did not have the coordination. His father would always help him back into the car. And neither would speak . . .
>
> It took nine months to graduate to pavement, and Arnold remembered the shock of the streets . . . The jarring sent shards of sensation—delayed, in his case, but real nonetheless, throughout his system. He had to quit after the first mile.[1]

Witherspoon's beautifully written narrative would bring a tear to the most cynical reader. One couldn't help but sympathize and admire the courageous young boy who, despite the advice of his doctor, parents, and friends, wanted to prove something. The article ended, saying: "They do not award prizes for bravery, for those who compete against the entire world instead of a stopwatch. If they had, in a field of 24,000, Arnold would have had no competition."

### Arnold Inspires Others

While readers were touched by the story (more than 100 contacted the newspaper following publication), the medical community was incredulous. They questioned the existence of this runner; others charged that even if Arnold did exist, publicizing the story gave false hope to cerebral palsy patients and encouraged them to do things that might destroy their already weakened bodies.

Two weeks later, Witherspoon's mid-week column carried a brief follow-up to the Arnold story. In four paragraphs at the end of another article, Witherspoon suggested that readers who were interested in Arnold's triumph contribute to the Cerebral Palsy Foundation. He then confessed that the story was "largely apocryphal. Arnold is a real person and his efforts to run in a mini-marathon—and his eventual success—were as described. But he did not run in Atlanta."[2]

That explanation did not satisfy everyone. And it stirred the ire of a writer for *Atlanta Magazine*, a monthly magazine that is filled with mostly upbeat articles on Southern life. Reporter Gail Dubrof looked further into the Arnold story; her investigation resulted in an exposé ("Reverberations of a Hoax") several months later. The article accused the newspaper of presenting fact as fiction; the July 21 clarification was described as "a further deception and a whitewash."[3]

Witherspoon defended his story, saying that a "column" differed from a news story and, therefore, allowed him more latitude for creativity than a straight news story. Witherspoon claimed that his account was based on an actual cerebral-palsied youth who ran a race in Iowa in 1973. One wonders why the paper chose the word apocryphal, which is defined by Webster as of "doubtful authenticity," if a boy such as Arnold did exist, as Witherspoon countinued to contend.

But Dubrof said Witherspoon repeatedly refused to provide *Atlanta Magazine* with details on the event such as a last name, a city where the race was held, or a newsclipping. Harold Yeglin, long-time sports editor of the *Des Moines Register,* told Dubrof that he "never heard anything like it."

## A Harmful Exaggeration

Besides giving false hope to cerebral palsy victims, and potentially causing them to harm themselves by engaging in inappropriate exercise, Witherspoon's article set for them an inappropriate standard—expectations that could never be realized.

A new type of journalism has surfaced in recent years that combines fact and fiction in order to tell a story. Perhaps the most notorious case was that of Janet Cooke of the *Washington Post,* who won (and later had revoked) the Pulitzer Prize for her series on Jimmy, a cocaine-addicted child. A similar community outcry in support of young Jimmy followed. Pressed to identify the boy, Cooke admitted Jimmy was a fictional character—a composite of many children who grow up in the poverty-drug culture. The intentions of both Cooke and Witherspoon were obviously altruistic. They desired that their stories would be inspirational and prompt action that would benefit the community in general.

Journalists can debate the difference between a news story and a news column, but for the lay reader the philosophical issue is meaningless. Their pain is real. They expect that the information they absorb from the news media is true. A column or news story about the heroics of an individual overcoming an illness or deformity has the same impact—it radiates hope. Journalists who write about heroics—be they real, apocryphal, or fictitious—must proceed cautiously because their readers, viewers, and listeners are vulnerable to the message.

Stories such as Witherspoon's apocryphal tale are more serious than a harmless exaggeration. When medical research is distorted—even when the intentions are noble—patients are given false hopes that can mislead them and cause physical damage. On a motivational level, embellished stories give patients a goal they cannot hope realistically to achieve. For many handicapped youngsters in Atlanta, they were told to ignore physical limitations and risk their health.

# 8 Selenium Story Put Cystic Fibrosis Sufferers at Risk

When C.P., an eleven-month-old girl with cystic fibrosis, was admitted to the University of Colorado Hospital in the summer of 1979, doctors knew immediately that her chances of survival were slim. She was pale, weighed less than twelve pounds, had an irregular heart beat, and suffered muscle spasms associated with a mineral imbalance. A battery of laboratory tests was ordered to determine the cause of her distress. As physicians waited for the test results, they placed the sick child on oxygen support and gave her antibiotics to combat possible infection. Within a few hours, she suddenly became unresponsive and went into shock. Despite vigorous resuscitation efforts, the little girl died five hours later.

C.P.'s tragic death inspired her doctors to warn other physicians—and the press—about the dangers of selenium as a treatment for cystic fibrosis. It seemed that C.P., a cystic fibrosis sufferer since shortly after her birth, had been taking selenium supplements for more than two months. Her physicians concluded that the selenium supplements in her diet may have caused her death.[1]

Why would anyone use selenium, a mineral obtained chiefly as a by-product of copper refining, to treat cystic fibrosis? According to her Colorado physicians, C.P. was given selenium "on the advice of a veterinarian."

## A Revolutionary Finding?

Dr. Joel Wallach, a veterinary pathologist, was working at the Yerkes Primate Research Center in Atlanta in 1977 when he came across what he believed was a revolutionary discovery regarding cystic fibrosis. In performing an autopsy of a monkey which had died mysteriously, he recognized tissue characteristic of cystic fibrosis. Analysis of the monkey's diet revealed a selenium deficiency.

Based on this one monkey, Wallach advanced the following theory: Cystic fibrosis is the result of a selenium deficiency and improper diet. This idea challenged a century of medical thought; the consensus being that cystic fibrosis was a hereditary illness. Within twenty-four hours of telling his superiors of this hypothesis, Wallach was out of a job at Yerkes. A few months later, Wallach went to the press with his claim of a cystic fibrosis cure; hundreds of newspapers carried the story. And by 1979, according to one published account, more than 150 patients had sought Wallach for vitamin treatment.

"I went public with this because I felt patients should know there is now an alternative. I am happy to be working with those who have volunteered for the program," Wallach told the *Hutchinson* (Kansas) *News*.[2] Stories about Wallach's "alternative treatment" also appeared in two wide circulation magazines—the *National Health Federation Bulletin*[3] and *Prevention*[4]—as well as subscribers of the UPI news service.

### Cystic Fibrosis: A Tragic Saga

More than thirty thousand people in the United States suffer from cystic fibrosis. Between fifteen hundred and two thousand children are born with the illness each year, making it the most common genetically transmitted disease in the United States—and definitely one of the cruelest—for there is no proven cure, and therapy is difficult and arduous. Half will die before they reach twenty-one, most of them suffering a lifetime of debilitating illness that involves uncontrollable coughing, lung congestion, and unrelenting infections.

Cystic fibrosis has many manifestations, but the most common symptom is the buildup of a thick, gummy mucus secreted through the body. The mucus primarily damages the lungs; about 95 percent of deaths are due to respiratory problems. The mucus also clogs the ducts of the pancreas, the organ which secretes enzymes vital to good digestion. This results in frequent malnutrition, a common cause of death in infants.

The consensus of the medical community, backed by an overwhelming abundance of scientific studies, asserts that cystic fibrosis is caused by a defective gene. It is a recessive gene, meaning that cystic fibrosis can occur in a person only when both parents carry it, although neither parent shows any symptom and both will live a normal life without any sign of cystic fibrosis. In families where two parents carry the cystic fibrosis gene, there's a one-in-four chance that their offspring will acquire two cystic fibrosis genes, and a one-in-two chance of receiving a single cystic fibrosis gene, and becoming a carrier.[5]

## Headlines Blare: Doctor Has Cure

Press reports of Wallach's theory gave new hope to thousands of young patients and their parents. Until then, cystic fibrosis victims had been told there was no cure because the disease was genetic and genetic engineering techniques that might hold out hope were still many years away.

Wallach attracted widespread news media attention by holding a press conference at Northwestern Memorial Hospital in Chicago on December 2, 1978. The UPI story based on that contrived news event was picked up by many American newspapers the next day, often under splashy headlines such as "Doctor Claims Cure for Cystic Fibrosis."[6] The story quoted only Wallach; there was no dissenting view from critical scientists or spokesmen for the Cystic Fibrosis Foundation, or NIH. In the UPI story, Wallach called his discovery "mind boggling." According to the wire service, "Wallach said tests in thousands of monkeys have shown the disease is 100 percent curable when diagnosed within 30 days of birth." The news story didn't cite Wallach's reference for such findings.

Other press accounts portrayed Wallach as an underdog, fighting against the medical establishment. Such was the story carried in the October 1979 issue of *Prevention* magazine, which claims the "largest circulation of any health magazine in the United States." The article, "Selenium: Hope for Cystic Fibrosis?" gave accounts of four patients who were following the Wallach diet and reporting positive results. A nineteen-year-old girl was quoted as saying: "When I used to get lung infections, they would last four or five days, and now they last only one or two." A mother said of her twenty-nine-month-old CF child: "His hair has become absolutely gorgeous and to look at Brent, nobody would know he even has cystic fibrosis."

The *Prevention* article's meager effort to present a balanced report consisted of a single comment from an official of the National Cystic Fibrosis Foundation, who cautioned: "I have not seen any hard, substantial evidence" to show that patients had been helped by the selenium supplement.

### Diet Gains a Following

At least 150 families believed Wallach's theory. They enrolled their children in his studies, or began giving selenium supplements without a physician's advice. Unknowingly, they were putting their children's lives at risk.

Wallach's selenium theory spurred an outcry from the scientific community. His theory was discussed at a "consensus conference" of physicians and scientists specializing in cystic fibrosis held at NIH in September 1979. The participants concluded there was no evidence to support the concept that selenium was a causative factor in cystic fibrosis or that it played a helpful role in routine treatment. The NIH meeting and its conclusions were not mentioned in the *Prevention* article, nor did it draw attention in the popular press.

"In particular, it was felt [at the conference] that the subjective improvement observed in some cystic fibrosis patients following dietary manipulation according to the recommendations of Dr. Wallach is probably related to more conscientious adherence to their diet and better compliance for attainment of recommended vitamins, minerals, and energy intakes," wrote three experts in an editorial in the *Journal of Pediatrics.*[7]

But what about the monkey which gave Wallach the initial clue to his cystic fibrosis theory? In their editorial, the three physicians—Dr. Van S. Hubbard of NIH, Dr. Giuilio Barbero of the University of Missouri, and Dr. H. Peter Chase of the University of Colorado Medical School—solved the mystery. They noted that "any relationship between selenium deficiency and the changes in this monkey were entirely hypothetical." Because no seleinum determinations were obtained on blood or tissue samples, the lesions observed on the monkey could have been due to a generalized malnutrition, the scientists surmised.

### Reporters Should Show Restraint

How should the press have treated the selenium story? In diseases of such potential gravity as cystic fibrosis, great responsibility rests on the shoulders of the news media to show restraint when communicating new ideas of therapy. In the news business, "restraint" is often interpreted as censorship. Many journalists bristle when the word is mentioned. They charge infringement of their First Amendment rights. Instead of a ban on medical news, what is needed is responsible reporting that may not be timely—from the newsman's perspective. By sacrificing timeliness, the press will find truth, which, in the long run, is more important.

For suffering patients, the distinction between truth and hypotheses frequently becomes clouded when hope for therapeutic benefit is so high. They develop the attitude that "there's nothing to lose, so I'll try it." But there is much to lose—precious time. And time might hold a real cure.

# 9 Laetrile: Media Hype of Pseudoscience

The story of laetrile is, simply, a story of medical quackery and pseudoscience carried to extreme heights by a well-orchestrated promotion campaign carried out, at least in part, through the news media. Laetrile was not the first quack cancer cure to flourish in the twentieth century, but "all prior forms of cancer quackery pale in comparison with the laetrile crusade, unquestionably the slickest, most sophisticated, and certainly the most remunerative cancer quack promotion in medical history," writes Dr. Irving J. Lerner, clinical associate professor of medicine at the University of Minnesota Medical School. [1]

## Laetrile: Born in a Basement

Laetrile's father of invention was Dr. Ernst Krebs, an obscure San Francisco physican, who first discovered the material in the 1920s. Rather than looking for a healing substance, Krebs was searching for an ingredient to improve the taste of bootleg whiskey. And he did it in his home—a basement laboratory!

Krebs believed that an extract of apricot seeds reduced the size of rodent tumors, but he warned that the chemical, known as amygdalin, was too dangerous for human use. The promotion of the substance as a miracle cure for human cancer began in the 1950s when his son, Ernst Krebs, Jr., claimed to have manufactured a safer form of the amygdalin, which he named laetrile. In 1963, the FDA refused to allow its interstate shipment, so laetrile users turned to clandestine sources to obtain the drug, made of ground apricot pits. Many traveled to clinics in Mexico, where government restrictions on laetrile use were less stringent than in the United States.

The news media's interest in laetrile heightened in the early 1970s as laetrile became a political as well as a medical issue. In 1970, Krebs claimed that he had traced the cause of all forms of cancer to a single cause—the unitarian theory of cancer—and that the disease was due to a vitamin deficiency. Krebs Jr. argued that the missing vitamin in cancer was laetrile, which he named vitamin $B_{17}$. Those ideas were discredited by the medical community while state and federal enforcement agencies began efforts to ban the sale of laetrile.

### The Media Sticks to the Story

The press was drawn to the laetrile story like a magnet. The laetrile controversy offered many story possibilities: dying patients going to desperate lengths to find a miracle potion; maverick scientists battling the bureaucracy; and a secret underground supply network. To some in the press, the story's social and ethical questions were more important than the scientific debate, which was actually one-sided—against the use of the fraudulent material.

News reports that included testimonials from patients claiming successful treatment helped spread the word of laetrile to other cancer patients. Some news stories were tempered with disclaimers from physicians, but other stories carried only patient accounts without comment from physicians. Laetrile promoters staged press conferences, including one on the steps of the Supreme Court. As laetrile promoters waved their flag and cited anecdotal successes, scientists and physicians did a poor job of countering the message; they were armed with "science" and statistics, which are not nearly as dramatic as the plight of human beings.

For Dr. Samuel G. Taylor, the media's portrayal of laetrile as even a possible cure for cancer was anathemic. Specifically, he was incensed over a series of reports on WBBM-TV, Chicago, that aired between January and September 1977. "No other TV station in this city has covered the laetrile issue with such bias and without any attempt to gather professional opinion or opposing arguments to its use," Taylor said in a complaint filed with the now-defunct National News Council. The News Council was formed in 1973 by interested laymen and journalists to investigate and judge specific complaints against the media.

Taylor, a member of the Northwestern University Medical School faculty, decided to challenge the news media after several of his cancer patients who had viewed the TV stories started taking laetrile. In his complaint, Taylor charged that the television station had overpromoted the story by interviewing three patients who claimed they had been cured of cancer and by using the word "breakthrough" to describe the substance.

In their defense, the TV station's producer and reporter noted that they had included several comments from physicians who disputed the healing powers of laetrile. And, in the final segment of a five-part series, there was the statement: "The physicians worry that someone might see the so-called miraculous cures and ignore accepted medical treatment. We share that fear and say frankly . . . Laetrile is no magic cure for cancer."

The News Council ruled that the television station had used the word "breakthrough" injudiciously, but found no merit in Dr. Taylor's other points. The News Council believed that the programs were balanced and gave adequate "representation to both sides involved in the continuing debate over laetrile."[2]

The problem here for the medical news consumer is that, medically speaking, the controversy was one-sided. Because no reputable scientists endorsed the use of laetrile, the press turned to testimonials in order to present the "other side of the story." Articles that attempted to explain the legal and medical controversy often began with an anecdote about a cancer victim's trip to Tijuana, Mexico, where the drug was available. Such was the case in the April 12, 1971, issue of *Time* magazine, one of the first articles on laetrile usage to appear in the lay press. It began:

> In a motel room in Imperial Beach, Calif., the thin man from Arizona puffed nervously on a cigarette as he told his story. Suffering from cancer of the lung, he was told last fall that he had only months to live. Two weeks ago, he came to Imperial Beach, and since then he has regularly driven across the border to Tijuana, Mexico, and visited a clinic where he receives a shot of Laetrile, a controversial drug that has been outlawed in the U.S. since 1963. Already, he claims to be better. Says he: "I feel now like I'm not going to die."[3]

Most news media paid scant attention to the drug until October 1973 when reports surfaced that Memorial Sloan-Kettering Cancer Center in New York City, one of the nation's leading medical research centers, was conducting secret tests of laetrile that looked promising. The first story appeared in the *Los Angeles Times*, which obtained a copy of preliminary research results on mice. According to the journal *Science*, the *Times* received the report from an attorney representing a California physician on trial for illegally administering laetrile. The scientific journal reported that the attorney "made a copy of the Slaon-Kettering reports available to medical reporter Harry Nelson of the *Los Angeles Times* in the hope that Nelson would write the story." Nelson had some doubts. In a later interview,[4] Nelson said he approached writing the story with trepidation because he knew that anything that he wrote would give credence to laetrile, and the evidence from Sloan-Kettering was weak. Nevertheless, Nelson indicated that, as a journalist, he felt compelled to write the story because the research was authentic. (In retrospect, Nelson said he was premature in reporting on the laetrile study. "I shouldn't have," he told an interviewer in 1977. "It was too soon. I should have waited for follow-up studies. But I wanted to be first with the story.")[5]

The *Times* story lighted a fire under other newsmen to pursue the story. Subsequently, the public information office at Sloan-Kettering was reportedly "bombarded with inquiries" from reporters on the West Coast seeking to develop their own versions of the laetrile story.

One of the first nationally televised news stories of the laetrile underground appeared on CBS-TV on May 29, 1975. The news feature began with the story of Ray and Myrtle en route to Tijuana and ended with cancer patient Joe Kehoe saying he would steal laetrile if necessary. The middle part of the story was devoted to the government's crackdown on smuggling of laetrile. Countering the U.S. Attorney's comments were those of a relative of a cancer patient who says she and many others like her were "willing to smuggle laetrile for someone they love."[6]

The scientific community's problems with laetrile—and press coverage of the story—were international. Two Israeli doctors described their experience in the July-August *Public Health Reports* following publication of a news story that claimed laetrile produced an 85 percent cure rate. "The effect of this article was shocking," wrote Drs. Zvi Fuks and Baruch Modan. "The public was extremely impressed, and people in Israel and abroad were anxiously calling the Israeli Ministry of Health for information on availability of the drug. Although the Ministry of Health discredited the claims, the power of the media was evident."[7]

## Testimonials Overshadow Truth

A scientist, even when armed with statistics and irrefutable data, is no match for a dying patient's testimonial. For the media, even an anecdotal story is considered legitimate information, as long as it is balanced with a differing point of view. The media can readily promote quack medicine by simply giving the quacks equal play in stories that portend to be balanced. Because cancer patients often feel helpless in the course of their disease, they are easily led to repudiate accepted facts and to grasp at straws of hope. People driven by fear are gullible; they are searching for the "miracle cure" and become susceptible to alternative treatments.

Because cancer is the chief health concern of more Americans than any other disease, the press must use extra caution in covering stories of new treatments. Even when the press is reporting on an apparently "quack" case, patients may be led to believe there is hope if they can obtain the magic remedy. Patients, especially terminally ill cancer sufferers, may feel they have nothing to lose by seeking unproven methods of treatment.

### Laetrile's Final Chapter

In August 1981, medical researchers announced the results of what was intended to be the definitive study of laetrile. Dr. Charles G. Moertel of the Mayo Clinic told the American Society of Clinical Oncology, and the American public via a news conference, that laetrile was ineffective in treating cancer. Neither did the drug shrink tumors, nor prevent cancers from seriously progressing, the study showed.

The story drew massive coverage, but some press organizations still gave attention to pro-laetrile groups. A survey of eighty-four American newspapers by the Office of Cancer Communications of NCI found that five newspapers gave unfavorable coverage to the results, quoting laetrile advocates who refuted the study.[8] The articles did not describe the study as definitive and said, "Laetrile advocates insist nothing was proved by human tests" or "a Government study branding laetrile as ineffective against cancer was labeled a farce today by a user of laetrile in cancer." Readers of these stories were led to believe that the controversy was unresolved and that the drug still held out hope. It didn't.

# 10 Cancer News Coverage

How well does the popular press cover cancer news? Judging from an extensive study by the Office of Cancer Communications at NCI, the answer is "not very well."

The NCI study, published in 1984, analyzed how the nation's fifty largest daily newspapers portrayed the cancer story during August, September, and October of 1980. Results were compared with a similar survey in 1977 to determine if there were any changes in trends of newspaper coverage of what the public considers "the most dreaded disease."[1]

Analysis of 1,466 articles revealed that American newspaper coverage of cancer:

• Presented a "fragmented and ephemeral picture" that concerned mostly fast-breaking events. In the case of complex scientific stories, this approach "may seriously affect the public's understanding of the disease," the researchers said.

• Lacked detailed information on cancer incidence rates, prevention and control. Prevention, or ways to minimize risk of contracting cancer, was the major cancer topic in only six percent of the news stories in 1980 (and only 4 percent in a 1977 survey). Detection was the major focus in only 3 percent of the stories.

• Failed to discuss cancer issues that the public is not well informed about. Many stories left readers with the erroneous notion that "everything causes cancer" and thus reinforced public fears. Colorectal cancer—a form of the disease that is highly treatable—was particularly underreported relative to the incidence of other types of cancer.

• Tended to emphasize dying rather than coping. Less than 5 percent of the news stories dealt with the many psychological, financial, or organizational resources available to help cancer patients and their families.

## Public Response to Cancer News

Cancer news, like no other medical story, provokes an emotional response from readers and viewers. This is probably because of cancer's pervasiveness and deadliness. Nearly half-a-million people die of cancer in the United States every year. The possibility of a new treatment that will prolong their lives means families will travel long distances and spend whatever it takes for the new miracle drug.

The experience following the March 28, 1976, article in *Parade* magazine, titled, "Does Your Doctor Know How to Treat Cancer?" illustrates how vulnerable the public is to cancer news. *Parade* is a Sunday supplement that appears in hundreds of newspapers throughout the country.

In the story, the writer described many recent advances in cancer treatment and concluded that, in his opinion, "the average cancer patient is likely to be misdiagnosed by his local doctor and maltreated in his local hospital." The author urged readers to seek a second medical opinion following diagnosis.

The public's reaction to the *Parade* article was studied by two researchers at the New York State Department of Health and the State University of New York at Buffalo—Robert W. Gerlach and Dr. Gerald P. Murphy.[2] They wondered if the story had any impact on patients entering Roswell Park Memorial Institute, one of the nation's top cancer research and treatment centers.

Of 1,166 responses to a questionnaire circulated to cancer patients at the hospital, 65 percent of them cited the newspaper article as a stimulant to seek a "cancer cure." The researchers stated:

> Although we cannot conclude whether the Parade article was the underlying cause of concern or only a stimulant that acted on existing concern, it is apparent that the written media can trigger an immediate response and have a measure of lasting influence on laymen concerned with cancer care . . . The vast majority of concern arises from layman insecurity regarding cancer care rather than disillusionment or implication of incompetency in community physicians.

### The Interleukin-2 Breakthrough

News of a "breakthrough" in the war on cancer surfaced in the popular press during the first week of December 1985. Massive media attention focused on an article in the *New England Journal of Medicine*.[3] Authored by NCI scientists, the article summarized their experience in treating cancer patients with a substance called interleukin-2. In these experiments, interleukin-2 was effective in eleven of twenty-five patients treated, but only one of the twenty-five patients had a complete disappearance of cancer. Ten others experienced only a partial disappearance or shrinkage of a primary tumor.

The story made the front page of newspapers across America, and led all four national television news programs. The following week, *Newsweek* made "Search for a Cure" its cover story.

What was the result of this saturation news coverage? Cancer patients across America flooded phone lines to the NCI, the National Cancer Information Service, and community hospitals, seeking access to the new wonder drug. Many patients wanted to volunteer to be participants in experimental studies. According to newspaper accounts, at least two patients.told their physicians that they were discontinuing their conventional therapy in hopes of getting interleukin-2.

Did interleukin-2 merit all of the attention? Dr. Evan Hersh of the M.D. Anderson Tumor and Cancer Institute in Houston, Texas, who was also experimenting with the drug, observed, "All this publicity is extremely unfortunate. The public needs to be informed about cancer research . . . But things have to be put into perspective and I think perspective has been lost on this."[4] Dr. Robert Mayer of the Dana-Farber Cancer Institute in Boston cautioned, "I would be very reluctant to put it up in neon lights and call it a major advance."

The story was overplayed by the news media, overpromoted by the scientists who held a press conference to coincide with publication in the medical journal, and misinterpreted by the public.

According to one journalist attending the NCI news briefing, "As he [the scientist] talked, the study got better in his own mind."[5] The next day, on NBC-TV's "Today" show, Dr. Steven Rosenberg called interleukin-2 the "first new kind of approach to cancer in perhaps twenty or thirty years," thus minimizing other advances in chemotheraphy and prevention.

Most press reports failed to point out how expensive the medication was, its side effects, and the fact that it was not available to the majority of cancer sufferers. The public was led to believe that they might soon benefit from interleukin-2.

The responsible media reports included comments from physicians who expressed doubts about interleukin-2. But the dissenting comments usually were buried several paragraphs into the story after news about the drug's success. Certainly, the NCI work was important but saturation coverage based on a short-term remission was not warranted, especially in view of the fact that treatment was available at only a few specialized cancer centers.

A year later, one of the nation's leading cancer researchers ripped both the press and the NCI scientists for misleading the public about interleukin-2. In an editorial in the *Journal of the American Medical Association (JAMA)* Dr. Charles G. Moertel of the Mayo Clinic questioned the use of the word "breakthrough" to describe preliminary results with the new drug. He compared the interleukin-2 press coverage to the "media extravaganza" that followed initial reports of the alpha-interferon a few years earlier. Those studies showed that interferon appeared to be an effective treatment for some of the same cancers that interleukin-2 seemed to suppress, but after years of study interferon has "an established clinical role in only one very rare type of leukemia," Moertel said.[6]

Referring to the NCI study, Moertel noted that the regression rate of 20 percent in cases of colorectal cancer is not unusual in small preliminary studies, and that some chemotherapeutic agents actually attain a regression rate of 80 percent in early studies, but are later discarded as inefffective after long-term in-depth studies.

The Mayo Clinic doctor believed media coverage of cancer treatments should be tempered because "any claim of therapeutic accomplishment will attract major public interest." In his editorial, Moertel also urged his scientific colleagues to "suppress the urge to publicly state or imply that a breakthrough has taken place until solid evidence exists that, indeed, there has been a breakthrough as the public would interpret it."

In analyzing the media's coverage of interleukin-2, science writer Ron Kotulak of the *Chicago Tribune* wrote in his column, "False Hopes Cloud Cancer Achievements": "Most scientists do not believe that a single magic bullet will ever be developed to cure all cancers. Yet every major advance tends to be greeted as a cure-all, often raising false hopes that can never be matched by reality."[7]

## Are We Really Winning the War on Cancer?

How accurate are media reports on cancer successes? A reading of press accounts of the war on cancer would lead one to believe that cancer patients are living significantly longer today than two decades ago thanks to major strides that have been made through new technologies, strategies for early detection, and powerful therapies. However, according to some researchers, the rosy picture painted by the news media is not based in fact. Despite a forty-fold increase in funding for cancer research from 1950 to 1982, age-adjusted cancer death rates actually went up 8 percent! In other words, whatever progress attained by better treatments has been abated by an increase in cancer incidence.

Two studies, both published in the *New England Journal of Medicine,* questioned the real success of this country's war on cancer. The reports indicated that survival rates for the most serious and widespread forms of cancer—lung, breast, colorectal, and prostate—have not really declined during the past two decades.

Researchers at Yale University compared two groups of patients with primary cancers of the lung—one group of patients who underwent initial treatment between 1953 and 1964, and the other first treated in 1977. They concluded that the apparently improved survival rates of the more recent group was a "statistical artifact" (something created by the way statistics are compiled and not a true reflection of reality).[8]

A more disturbing criticism followed about a year later in the May 20 issue of the *Journal* by John C. Bailar III of Harvard's School of Public Health, and Dr. Elaine M. Smith of the University of Iowa Medical Center. In their article, "Progress Against Cancer," these researchers said:

Age-adjusted mortality rates have shown a slow and steady increase over several decades, and there is no evidence of a recent downward trend. In this clinical sense we are losing the war against cancer . . . The main conclusion we draw is that some 35 years of intense effort focused largely on improving treatment must be judged a qualified failure. Results have not been what they were intended and expected to be.[9]

The two epidemiologic studies drew criticism from cancer groups and doctors who argued that the statistical reviewers did not judge the quality of survival, and that the analysts included selection biases. The press's role has been to report information presented by groups such as the American Cancer Society and NCI. In this case, the press may have been only a pawn in the manipulation game.

## Pseudo-Cancer Report Misleads Patients

In 1982 and 1983, several news media, including the *New York Times*[10] and the *St. Paul Dispatch*,[11] carried fascinating medical detective stories about a pseudo-cancer. The stories, which resulted from a news release issued by the Public Relations Office at the University of Minnesota, described the discovery of a new disease that mimicked the behavior of cancer, but actually was not a malignant disease.

The disease was called RAH, for Regressing Atypical Histiocytosis: "regressing" because the tumors eventually go away, often without treatment; "atypical" because of the unusual behavior; and "histiocytosis" for the type of white cell in which the disease originates, a histiocyte, a scavenger cell that seeks out and destroys foreign material that invades the body. Such occurrences are called "pseudo-cancers."

In discussing his discovery, Dr. Kevin J. Flynn, who was completing a post-graduate fellowship in dermatology at the time, emphasized the mysterious nature of the disease. He speculated that, in the long run, people who suffer from

RAH may, indeed, still have cancer. His discovery was based on only a few patients, including a sixty-four-year-old man and a ten-year-old girl, who had been treated at University of Minnesota Hospital. Flynn and his colleagues reported their findings to the scientific community in the journal *Cancer* in March 1982.[12] The article resulted in dozens of tissue samples from doctors around the world; only a few turned out to be RAH.

News media coverage of RAH spurred another kind of reaction from patients following the news stories. Flynn began receiving telephone calls and letters from patients who had real cancers yet wanted to believe that they had RAH and, as a result, were planning to discontinue their cancer therapy.[13]

Although both the *Dispatch* and *Times* stories included Flynn's cautionary comments, they apparently had little impact on readers who chose to self-diagnose themselves as sufferers of "pseudo-cancers" rather than real malignancies. Flynn said that he was overwhelmed by calls from patients who believe they had RAH and believed, erroneously from the news accounts, that he could somehow treat them.

# 11 Herpes Hysteria

What caused the widespread fear of genital herpes? Was the so-called "herpedemic" as pervasive and as contagious as the news media led us to believe?

Much of the blame for the public paranoia of herpes rests with the press. In the early 1980s, print and electronic media were saturated with news and feature stories about the new sexual disease that infects between three hundred thousand and five hundred thousand people a year. Sensationalized articles focused on pain, emotional suffering, birth defects in babies, and the apparent helplessness of the medical community to find a cure.

In covering the epidemic, many news media parlayed the illness into scare stories that exaggerated the danger far beyond its actual threat. This chapter examines two incidents that contributed to the public hysteria.

## Tiniest Organism in the Universe

Herpes is a virus—the tiniest organism in the world that may be called alive. It has been around for centuries and may be one of the world's most common viruses. In medical nomenclature, herpes used by itself represents a family of five different but related human viruses: herpes simplex virus type 1 (HSV-1), the most common cause of cold sores; herpes simplex virus type 2 (HVS-2), the most common cause of genital herpes; Epstein-Barr virus, the cause of mononucleosis; varicella-zoster virus, the cause of chickenpox in children

93

and shingles in the elderly; and cytomegalovirus, which infects 90 percent of the population but only causes problems in cancer and transplant patients and for some neonates.[1]

Because of space and time limitations, the press must use concise language. In the case of herpes, the word was most often used to describe the epidemic of venereal disease associated with HSV-2, although technically herpes can be applied to the family of five viruses. As we shall see later in this chapter, word confusion led directly to problems in a Baltimore elementary school which caused the ostracism of a young boy.

## The Hot Tub Debate Debacle

When a scientist releases information, it is not always definitive. Often, it is done to inspire further research. The scientist may have found only one small piece of the puzzle. Preliminary reports in medical journals serve to interest other scientists to enter the research arena. Sometimes, the popular press intervenes in this process. Medical reporters from television and newspapers have a tendency to focus on one article, and rarely develop the long-term perspective. The following story illustrates the problem.

In the December 9, 1983, issue of *JAMA* appeared results of a study titled, "Survival of Herpes Simplex Virus in Water Specimens Collected from Hot Tubs in Spa Facilities and on Plastic Surfaces." The authors were laboratory pathologists at NIH.

The thesis of the four-page article was summarized in the last sentence of the abstract, ". . . survival of significant amounts of virus for 4.5 hours on plastic surfaces suggests that fomites such as these may be nonvenereal routes for HSV transmission."[2] The key word here is "nonvenereal," meaning nonsexual transmission. This idea ran counter to the consensus of the medical community, which believed that transmission occurred only through genital contact. The possibility of nonvenereal transmission that did not require direct bodily contact would have a significant public health impact.

Also in the December 9 issue of *JAMA* was an editorial that commented on the study results. Its authors, Drs. John M. Douglas and Lawrence Corey of the University of Washington at Seattle, run one of the nation's largest herpes clinics. In a kindly way, their editorial cast serious doubt upon the NIH study. They said: "While Nerurkar and others have demonstrated that HSV can survive on wet cloth or plastic for several hours . . . these observations do not provide proof that fomites play a role in the transmission of genital herpes."[3]

According to the Seattle doctors, the NIH study did not make sense based on their own extensive epidemiological experience at the University of Washington. In their work with 502 patients suffering first episodes of genital herpes, Douglas and Corey found that all were sexually active and all but 11 reported intercourse within the previous four weeks of being enrolled as a patient in their sexual disease clinic.

Their most incisive comment came in the last paragraph of the editorial: "The ability of HSV to survive on fomites makes commonsense precautions about care in the intimate sharing of wet surfaces or cloth reasonable. More cogent advice, however, would be the paraphrase of an anonymous piece of bathhouse graffiti, that 'more important than what's next to a hot tub is what goes on inside it.' " In other words, Douglas and Corey were questioning the activities of hot tub users.

The *Chicago Tribune*, the nation's third largest newspaper, ran the following news article about the hot tub study.

The virus that causes genital herpes is able to survive long enough on the plastic surfaces of hot tub benches to infect bathers, researchers at the National Institutes of Health have found.

While this does not prove that genital herpes is being spread without sexual intercourse, it does mean such a thing is at least theoretically possible.

The research by federal scientists reported in the Journal of the American Medical Association published today, was undertaken after several spas in the Washington, D.C., area complained of contracting genital herpes without sexual involvement.

The federal studies of hot tub spas, headed by Dr. Lata S. Nerurkar of the National Institutes of Health, found that the herpes virus didn't survive in chemically treated hot tub water but could live for several hours on plastic coated benches and seats near hot tubs.

The persistence of virus on plastic suggests that these surfaces might provide a route for nonvenereal spread of herpes simplex virus. They concluded, "This is of particular interest, since several spas were temporarily closed because patrons reported getting genital herpes simplex virus infection following the use of their facilities."[4]

The remainder of the news story summarized two other *JAMA* articles: one that cited an alarming increase in the number of babies born with neonatal herpes; and another on the development of a new test to tell if a person is shedding the virus.

In the *New York Times* account, the lead paragraph told of the surge in newborns with herpes. The second paragraph contained a "second lead" that introduced the hot tub study, which was elaborated on later in the story as follows:

A report in the Journal by researchers at the National Institutes of Health at Bethesda, Md., said several health clubs in the Washington, D.C., area had been closed because of the fear that some customers had been infected by herpes viruses transmitted through water in hot tubs . . .

These sources must be considered as important possible routes for nonvenereal spread of herpes virus, the group reported. The senior author of its report was Dr. Lata S. Nerurkar of the National Institutes of Health of Neurologic and Communicative Disorders and Stroke.[5]

NBC-TV covered the story on the evening news of Thursday, December 8, 1983. The story, read by anchorman Tom

Brokaw, went as follows: "Scientists now believe that you can catch herpes from hot tubs. According to a report in tomorrow's edition of the Journal of the American Medical Association, herpes virus will survive up to 4.5 hours on plastic benches."[6]

Neither the *Chicago Tribune, New York Times* nor NBC stories mentioned the accompanying editorial, nor did any of the three media outlets quote scientists who discounted the NIH report.

Drs. George J. Pazin and James H. Harger of the University of Pittsburgh School of Medicine felt the hot tub research was flawed, and that news coverage contributed to further public misunderstanding. In a letter to *JAMA* they said that while there is a theoretical possibility of nonsexual transmission, their extensive experience with genital herpes patients showed that it was "so rare as to be practically nonexistent. If nonsexual acquisition of genital herpes were a significant problem, we would expect to see occasional persons acquire genital herpes without being sexually active. We do not."[7] As far as the news coverage of the hot tub study, they said the misleading articles had caused people to lose jobs and to waste money on expensive antiseptics to clean toilet seats.

Because of the extensive public paranoia about genital herpes, the news media was obligated to make sure that it was presenting a balanced view of how the medical community felt about methods of transmission. A few news media, such as the *Washington Post*, did attempt to give a balanced account. Unfortunately, the headline of the story, "Herpes Virus Can Contaminate Hot Tub Areas, Journal Says," failed to accurately capture the sense of the story.[8]

**The Nightline Debacle**

In January 1985, a three-year-old boy attending a suburban

Baltimore school became the center of national media attention when parents of his classmates kept their youngsters home because they were afraid of herpes transmission. ABC-TV News "Nightline" devoted two broadcasts to herpes in the school: on Friday, January 11, in a segment titled, "Children with Herpes," and again on the following Monday, January 14, in a report titled: "Children and Herpes: How Great a Danger?" Why two consecutive stories on the same subject? Host Ted Koppel explained it this way when he introduced the Monday night segment.

We have rarely, if ever, done this before. But our program last Friday evening on the subject of herpes and children apparently succeeded in raising more questions than it answered and alarming more people than it reassured. Those of you who didn't see the broadcast, don't worry, you're probably better off. Those of you who did, give us another chance, we're about to try it again.[9]

The Friday evening broadcast began with a background story by correspondent Jed Duvall, who interviewed the boy's mother, a school official, and Dr. Stephen Straus, a scientist at the CDC. Straus's comments should have been enough to quell the story. He said: "I don't think there's a necessity for alarm in the community if there is a teacher of anyone else with herpes. Most people, in fact, get herpes infections early in childhood—that's the most common time to get it. By middle age about 70 percent of us have been infected with the virus (HSV-1). That means over 160 million Americans have been infected with this virus and carry it in their bodies for life."[10]

Duval nicely summarized the report as follows: "Same old problem, cold sores, with a new label, herpes. Millions are afflicted. One of them is Johnny Bigley. But the youngster is one of just a few, very few, in the center of much confusion, misinformation, and unmanageable fear." Duval's summation foretold the next twenty minutes of the "Nightline" broadcast, for when Ted Koppel and his guests returned, they muddied the waters to such an extent that the Monday night clarification segment was mandated.

What happened?

Among Koppel's guests on Friday were a parent, who was keeping his child home, and a leading herpes expert from Emory University Medical School in Atlanta. On several occasions, the scientist seemed to confuse Koppel (and the audience?) by giving exhaustive detail about the human herpes family of five viruses. Meanwhile, the parent offered incorrect information. At one point, the parent claimed that he had seen no scientific data to minimize risks, although the scientific literature abounded with it.

The Monday evening clarification broadcast featured Dr. Timothy Johnson, ABC-TV's medical correspondent who excels in explaining hard scientific information in easy-to-understand terms. The program was a vast improvement over the Friday night debacle. Koppel concluded the segment, stating: "There is no way that we are going to be able to answer all of the questions here tonight, and I'm sure we haven't. But I hope at least we have put it in somewhat better perspective than we did on Friday. . . ."

### A Forum for Misinformation

Allowing laymen to speak as medical authorities serves to spread misinformation. And scientists who are not adept speakers can also confuse the public by being too technical in their comments. The news media has neither the time nor, in many cases, the ability to screen its interviewees regarding their level of expertise and communication ability. As a result, the public suffers.

# 12 Acupuncture and Hearing Loss

We had tried everything for our hearing-impaired son Tommy when I heard about acupuncture treatment. I couldn't find anyone to do it here, but a friend had heard of a clinic in Washington. Both Tommy's audiologist and pediatrician discouraged us from going, and several friends, who are also parents of hearing-impaired children, said I was crazy. But they also asked me to call them right away if it worked.

—A Minneapolis mother

In 1973, an unusual article by Dr. Alfred Peng detailing acupuncture treatment for deafness appeared in the premiere issue of the *American Journal of Chinese Medicine*.[1] It was quickly followed by sensational news stories in the popular press that sent shock waves through the audiological profession while raising the hopes of many parents, such as this Minneapolis mother, with hearing-impaired youngsters.

The news stories claimed that profoundly deaf patients with sensorineural hearing loss (sometimes called "nerve deafness") had been restored to normal hearing through the ancient Oriental technique of acupuncture—the placing of tiny pins in various parts of the body. In this application, pins were placed in six vital points around the ear. The great majority of physicians and scientists were skeptical of the technique.

## Press Promotes Needles

Among the news organizations promoting acupuncture

treatment were the *New York Times* (February 26, 1973), *Newsweek* magazine (March 12, 1973), and UPI (September 12, 1973). Attention-grabbing headlines such as "Acupuncture Cures Nerve Deafness for Floridian"; "Needles Open New Worlds"; "Acupuncture Is Used to Help Save Victims of Nerve Deafness"; and "Acupuncture Holds New Hope for Nerve Deaf" led readers to believe that acupuncture was a medically accepted procedure when, in fact, its true effectiveness was still very much in doubt.

As a result of the extensive press attention, patients began requesting acupuncture treatments. One medical journal reported a "phenomenal surge" in demand for the procedure.[2] Twelve acupuncturists in the Washington, D.C., area began offering deafness treatment, drawing patients "from widely scattered parts of the United States," according to news reports.

News stories were based on Peng's four hundred-word article in the *American Journal of Chinese Medicine*. Peng, of New York's St. Luke's Hospital, claimed that eight of ten patients undergoing acupuncture treatment showed some degree of improvement. The most remarkable change occurred in a fifty-three-year-old woman who had been deaf for twenty-nine years, he said. After fourteen acupuncture treatments, the woman was able to hear sounds previously audible only with a hearing aid. Peng warned that his patients had been followed for only six months and that it was too early to say whether the improvement would be permanent.

Was acupuncture a panacea, or the answer to the prayers of thousands of hearing-impaired people? To resolve the growing controversy between acupuncturists and audiologists, scientists in the United States and Canada undertook two studies to test whether acupuncture was a viable treatment. One inquiry was a retrospective look at patients by a group of hearing professionals in Washington, D.C. The second study by the Department of Otolaryngology at the University of Toronto actually tested new patients with acupuncture under controlled conditions.

A close reading of Peng's article shows that he never intended his report to precipitate a radical change of standard audiology therapy. Indeed, he called his work "preliminary," designed primarily to introduce acupuncture to an American medical audience. The article was only three and one-half pages in length, including a one-page drawing of acupuncture points on the skull and another page of two audiograms.

After examining Peng's article, the Otolaryngology Section of the Medical Society of Washington, D.C, concluded the study was "void of scientific merit." The Society noted Peng's tests were done by different methods, and the report lacked essential details such as the dates of testing. Also, it appeared that the author considered 80 percent loss the same as 80dB (decibel) loss. In comparing audiograms from before and after acupuncture of sixty-six deaf patients who had undergone needle treatment, they concluded that acupuncture was a "most questionable remedy" for deafness.[3]

Meanwhile, twenty-nine deaf patients ranging in age from eighteen to seventy at the University of Toronto underwent acupuncture treatment under strict laboratory conditions. The acupuncturist, an accredited master who taught the technique in Taiwan, was flown to Toronto to perform the procedure. He had claimed success in using acupuncture for deafness in Taiwan.

The patients were divided into groups—some receiving acupuncture at sites supposed to affect hearing loss, and others at inactive points. Patients received two treatments a week, and none knew to which group he or she was assigned until the end of the experiment. In comparing the two groups, the scientists found that acupuncture did not affect hearing in adults with hearing loss in both ears. Gains in one ear were balanced by losses at another. No patients showed a "steady gain" in hearing throughout the course of therapy.

At the conclusion of the study, the researchers said they failed to observe a "clinically significant shift in hearing either during the course of or after treatment. . . . These findings lead us to conclude that acupuncture is not an effective form of treatment for sensorineural hearing loss."[4]

Neither study refuting acupuncture treatment for deafness attracted news media interest.

### Press Fails at Follow-up

One problem with news coverage of medical developments is that the media is "event centered." The acupuncture story was linked to a timely event—the debut of a new journal. The follow-up research that discounted its effectiveness deserved news media attention in order to set the record straight. This lack of follow-through, which is a frequent criticism of journalism in general, can be particularly dangerous in the medical arena where whole bodies of information may be overlooked because they did not come to the attention of a reporter.

But what about Peng's miracle patient—the fifty-three-year-old woman who allegedly improved after twenty-nine years of deafness? Remember, it was this woman's story that ignited the public interest in the first place. Although Peng claimed she had undergone "considerable improvement," a close reading of the article reveals that she had improved to an "80 percent hearing loss" after fourteen treatments during a three-month period, meaning she was still profoundly deaf by audiological standards. All of the hoopla, then, was based on a 20 percent hearing improvement measured by suspect technique!

Parents of sick and handicapped children are particularly vulnerable to any medical discovery that shows the slightest sign of worth. Many of those who traveled to Washington were parents of hearing-impaired children who desperately wanted to communicate with their children. They feel it is their duty to leave no stone unturned in the quest to help their child. The best advice is to temper your hopes with realistic expectations. Ignore stories based on so-called preliminary reports in medical journals until they have been verified by other sources and endorsed by medical professionals whom you respect.

# 13 The Vasectomy Scare

In the process of medical science, theories are often tested on animals in order to give insight into the human condition. Although there are many good reasons to experiment with animals, results in humans may differ. A drug that produces a particular effect in a rodent sometimes reacts differently in a human being. Therefore, when scientists report their findings based on animal studies, the work is routinely considered preliminary, intended to help guide future experiments. The ultimate test must be done with humans.

The lay press can mislead the public by reporting extensively on animal research results without mentioning its limitations. This exposure gives unwarranted credibility to the work—often far more than what the scientist originally intended. Such was the case in 1978 when Dr. Nancy J. Alexander of the Oregon Primate Research Center and a colleague issued their findings of the effect of vasectomies in monkeys.[1]

## Monkey Study Spurs News Coverage

On March 30, 1978, Alexander and Dr. Thomas B. Clarkson of the Bowman Gray School of Medicine at Wake Forest University in North Carolina, presented a brief report at the annual meeting of the American Fertility Society. The scientists had studied ten male cynomologus monkeys, a species of *Macaca* whose physiological response to dietary cholesterol closely resembles that of human beings. Five monkeys had been vasectomized; the other five were not, in order to serve as controls. When the monkeys were sacrificed, researchers found that the five vasectomized monkeys had evidence of an acceleration of atherosclerosis (hardening of arteries and veins), a major risk factor in heart disease and strokes.

If such findings were true in humans, they would affect a significant population of American men. Between 1968 and 1978, an estimated twelve million American men opted for the procedure, making it the most common method of sterilization for men. A vasectomy is a relatively simple twenty-minute procedure, usually performed in a physician's office with local anesthetic. It involves removal of part of the vas deferens—the duct that transfers sperm from the testicle to the male sex organ.

Alexander's brief presentation drew extensive newspaper coverage, including articles in the *New York Times* and *Washington Post*. Although both the *Post* and *Times* stories carried qualifying comments and the word "preliminary," the news slant indicated that this was an important story for readers because the finding *might* also apply to humans.

The ten-paragraph *Washington Post* article included the following interpretive comment: "The study suggests that men genetically inclined to heart attacks or strokes either watch their diet or not have vasectomies or both."[2] The statement was not attributed to anyone; it was the reporter's observation. In the very next paragraph, Dr. Alexander discounted that observation. "It is impossible to confirm even that much within certainty until further studies are done."

The fifteen-paragraph *New York Times* article, which focused primarily on study methods, was topped by the headline: "Monkey Vasectomies Hint Harm to Artery." The lengthy story included a single disclaimer: "The researchers emphasized that their findings could not yet be used to implicate vasectomy in human beings as a factor in human atherosclerosis.

Much more research would have to be done both to confirm the link in animals and to see whether it holds in people."[3]

While the newspapers had speculated that men might be at some risk from the operation, Alexander told the *Post* reporter there was no evidence to draw that conclusion. "We are not saying stop vasectomies today. These findings are preliminary," she said.

### Patients Alarmed

Dr. Robert Benjamin, a Minneapolis surgeon who had been performing vasectomies since 1961 at a rate of several hundred a year, said a number of his patients called to voice concern after reading newspaper accounts of the vasectomy-heart disease study. "They were worried. I did my best to allay their concerns." Benjamin said that he had seen enough patients in his practice to know that there was no link to heart disease. Surgeons in other parts of the country faced similar responses from their patients, Benjamin said.[4]

Although the medical community expressed some concern after the Alexander report, there was no call for a ban against the surgery. "Those who have had a vasectomy should just forget it [the monkey study]," Gustav Nossal, an eminent Australian immunologist, said. Dr. Roy LeRiche, an officer of the Alberta College of Physicians and Surgeons, "There is absolutely no evidence that anything has happened, or will happen, to men" who undergo the operation.[5]

### ·Press Downplays Definitive Studies

In 1983 and 1984, several studies were published in the scientific literature that proved vasectomies were safe in human beings. Two of them were extensive, epidemiologicial surveys of more than ten thousand vasectomized men who were compared with an age-matched control group who had not undergone the procedure. Here's what the researchers found: Vasectomy does *not* predispose men to coronary heart disease or cancer.[6] Interestingly, non-vasectomized men had a 50 percent higher overall death rate and twice the cancer death rate compared with men who underwent the operation. In other words, the men who had undergone the surgery seemed to be in better general health and lived longer than non-vasectomized men. Further, there was no apparent link between the surgery and any major disease, including cancer, heart disease, asthma, arthritis, and epilepsy.

How did the *Times* and *Post* cover the vasectomy-in-man research? The *Times* story was three paragraphs in length, compared to the original article of fifteen paragraphs, and was placed in the newspaper's "Science Watch Column," a roundup of several short items. The *Post's* follow-up story was four paragraphs long and placed as the second item of a similar news summary.

### Press Walks a Tightrope

Reporters who attend scientific conferences walk a tightrope. In the meeting halls and seminar rooms, they hear scientists present exciting new information on research results. But the presentations include caveats. News stories may include cautionary comments from the scientist, such as Alexander's admonition that she was not suggesting that vasectomies be banned. But these statements are usually placed toward the bottom of the story, and never in the lead paragraph. Caveats are often left out of television and radio news altogether.

A second problem in stories such as this is the manner in which newspapers follow up with rebuttal or contradictory information months or years following the first big splash of news and scare headlines. Such reports usually receive only scant attention and may be buried back in the paper or in roundup columns.

## News Consumers Need Another View

The press, of course, is not going to curtail reporting preliminary research. So how should news consumers react to such medical news? If the story involves a medical condition of interest to you, obtain a copy of the original article and read it for yourself to see if the scientist was speculating on how the reasearch might affect humans. In addition, check for other published articles. Scientists often disagree through the letters columns of medical journals, although rebuttals are sometimes delayed by several months because of the lengthy production schedule of scientific journals.

# 14 Sweet News for Diabetics?

Diabetes takes a heavy toll on the ten million Americans who suffer from this chronic disorder. They face a lifetime of cautious dieting and endure a greater risk of heart disease and stroke. Limb amputation is sometimes necessary. Complications from the disease account for approximately 130,000 deaths every year. Any news report on diabetes research will automatically generate widespread interest.

**Diabetes Primer**

Diabetes comes in two forms, commonly referred to as Type I and Type II. Type I, also called juvenile-onset or insulin-dependent diabetes, usually strikes children and infants and accounts for roughly 15–20 percent of all cases. Type II diabetes generally strikes in middle age; it does not require insulin injections. In both cases, the disease involves a failure of the body's natural regulation of glucose, our body's major fuel. Normally, glucose levels are controlled by insulin, a hormone produced in the pancreas. But in diabetes, the pancreas either doesn't produce enough insulin, or what is produced is not used properly by the body. Glucose then spills into the urine, drawing water from the body so it can be excreted. Eventually, this abnormality damages nerves, arteries, and organs.

To stave off those complications, diabetics must closely monitor their diets to maintain stable insulin levels. It is believed that fluctuations in insulin levels lead to nerve dam-

110

age. Weight loss and diets high in protein and fiber can reduce insulin requirements.

For nearly sixty years, physicians advised diabetics to carefully control their blood sugar, fearing that excessive intake would cause a significant increase in blood-sugar levels. Two scientific studies on ice cream in the diets of diabetics that appeared in the medical literature in 1983 and 1984 gave new hope to patients that they might be able to loosen up their restrictive diets.

Both the 1983 article, published in the *New England Journal of Medicine*,[1] and the 1984 report in *JAMA*[2] drew widespread media coverage. Each report was accompanied by an editorial that attempted to put the study into context; both studies, and both editorials, said more research was necessary before diabetics should begin changing their diet. But that was not the message some of the popular press conveyed.

### Minnesota Study: Press Missed the Qualifiers

The *New England Journal of Medicine*, published weekly, has an audience of nearly three hundred thousand physicians throughout the world. Journalists may also subscribe on the condition that they recognize the embargo date, which is 6:00 P.M. EST for television on the Wednesday night before the Thursday publication date. It may appear in Thursday morning newspapers. Journalists and physicians usually receive their copies on Monday or Tuesday of the week. The lead time allows physicians to prepare for possible questions from patients. For reporters, those two days provide valuable time to prepare well-balanced reports by interviewing the principal authors and other experts in the field for their consenting or dissenting views.

Despite the advance notice, not every media outlet covered the sugar research with the depth required of such a sensitive story. Such was the case in the news story that appeared in *USA Today*, with a readership of more than two million, on July 7, 1983, under the headline: "SUGAR: Study OKs It for Diabetics."

There's no evidence that eating sugar is harmful to diabetics, a study released today finds—contradicting years of conventional wisdom.

For years doctors have recommended that diabetics stay away from simple sugars such as sucrose, and instead eat a diet rich in complex carbohydrates, found in vegetables, fruits and grains. They have also recommended that diabetics substitute artificial sweeteners for sugar.

The study in today's New England Journal of Medicine found no difference in blood sugar levels after a sucrose meal and complex carbohydrate meals in a group of diabetics and healthy subjects.

Doctors have thought blood sugar levels rose following sugar intake. A diabetic can't control those levels.

Alice Perkins, a nutritionist with the American Diabetes Association, advises the USA's 11 million diabetics to moderate their sugar intake.

There's more evidence that sugar may not be bad, but diabetics need to keep in mind that it's still empty calories. Carbohydrates from fruits and vegetables are better.[3]

This six-paragraph story illustrates one of the most grievous errors of medical reporting in the popular press: the failure to include qualifiers. In this case, the qualifier was extremely important for, without it, diabetics could be put at risk. In the study, scientists from the University of Minnesota found that diabetics could use sugar but only when it was consumed in the context of a well-balanced meal.

Dr. John P. Bantle, assistant professor of medicine and lead author of the study, emphasized this point repeatedly during a news conference that was hurriedly called to explain the results after reporters began inundating his office with requests for interviews.

At the news conference, Bantle urged the press to treat his

work cautiously because of its preliminary nature. "This is a single study and before putting faith in its conclusions I think it would be important to see if similar results can be obtained by other investigators. And secondly, if there are to be changes made in diet recommendations for diabetics, these changes should be recommended by the Committee for Food and Nutrition of the American Diabetes Association."[4]

### Docs Feared Media Mixup

Less than a year after Bantle's research went public, similar results by researchers at Massachusetts General Hospital and Harvard University drew another barage of publicity following publication in *JAMA* of the article titled, "Ice Cream in the Diet of Insulin-Dependent Diabetic Patients."

In their study, the scientists found that consumption of a small amount of ice cream—the equivalent of a three-quarter cup serving—showed only a moderate increase in blood sugar levels, if a small dose of insulin were given thirty minutes before the meal. The study group was small, only ten insulin-dependent diabetics. Five relied on once- or twice-a-day insulin injections and five who used implanted pumps or multiple injections.

In their *JAMA* article, the Harvard scientists urged caution.

The results of our study should not be construed as giving license to the diabetic patient to ingest either ice cream or other desserts with sucrose freely. The importance of incorporating previously "forbidden" ice cream into a weight-maintaining diet must be stressed. It does seem, however, that ice cream can be ingested in moderate quantities and, with insulin coverage, does not adversely affect acute glucose control.

Dr. David M. Nathan, chief author of the report, later commented that he expected a media barrage to follow the published report and tried to stem the tide by answering reporters' phone calls. Although he felt the majority of media coverage was accurate, many news reports were misinterpreted by the reading, viewing, and listening public. For months, Nathan continued to hear from patients who told him that they believed it was okay to eat sweets.

Such a reaction was feared by Dr. David J.A. Jenkins of the University of Toronto who wrote an editorial that accompanied Nathan's article. Jenkins said:

> . . . adherence to most therapeutic diets is difficult. In both U.S. and British studies, a substantial proportion of diabetic patients were found not to be adhering to a diabetic diet. Today the majority of people are not noted for such conservative virtues as restraint, moderation, and balance. Obesity remains a major problem, and one with special implications for the diabetic population. Great care must therefore be taken in how the results of these studies are presented to the public through the media.[5]

The *JAMA* article attracted extensive media attention. In some news accounts, it was treated as a brand new finding, "Breakthrough for Diabetics Reported," although similar information had been reported by Bantle's group nearly a year earlier.

### Different Time Tunnels ˎ

The fact that scientists and journalists perceive the world through different time tunnels was evident in these stories. The scientists, in calling for long-term studies, would have preferred to await further documentation before announcing their findings to the public. Bantle and his colleagues based their conclusions on only twenty diabetic patients; Nathan's group studied only ten. Bantle said: "I think it's important to see if these results hold up in the hands of other investigators because, in fact, it is possible that our conclusions will be wrong. . . ."

Actually, those conclusions proved to be correct and in December 1984, the American Diabetes Association announced that it was revising its dietary recommendations to say that a "modest amount" of sugar is acceptable for diabetics. The ADA said the action was based on new studies, including the Minnesota and Harvard work.

For diabetics, however, there was no license to eat sugar outside the parameters of their recommended diets. Unfortunately, that was the impression some of the early news reports had given.

# 15 Whooping Cough Makes a Comeback

In April 1982, a Washington, D.C., television station aired an hour-long documentary that claimed to expose the dangers of the vaccine to prevent whooping cough. Titled "DPT: Vaccine Roulette," the program by WRC-TV included dramatic pictures of brain-damaged children, writhing in discomfort, and emotion-laden comments from their anguished parents. An eleven-minute segment of the WRC-TV documentary appeared the next morning on NBC's nationwide "Today" show, reaching millions of parents across America, and sending thousands of them to consult health departments and physicians to question the safety of DPT.

Reacting to the exaggerated and sensationalized dangers, many parents have refused to allow their children to undergo vaccine inoculation out of fear that their child will experience adverse and possibly irreversible side effects. Since that documentary, ten states have reported an increase in pertussis cases and the publicity surrounding the vaccine may be partly responsible for the increase, according to some experts.[1]

## A Most Deadly Disease

In medicine, whooping cough is called pertussis and represents the P in the DPT vaccine. Usually given to infants in a series of three shots beginning at three months of age, DPT is considered part of standard well-baby care. (The D is for Diptheria and T represents the vaccine for Tetanus.)

Pertussis was once among the most deadly and infectious

of all childhood diseases in the United States. In the 1940s, about six thousand children died every year from whooping cough, while thousands of others suffered through the horrible disease, experiencing pneumonia, encephalitis, respiratory distress, and brain damage.

The following description from *Taber's Cyclopedic Medical Dictionary* gives a graphic picture of exactly how devastating the disease can be to young children.

*Pertussis*—an acute, infectious disease characterized by a catarrhal stage, followed by a peculiar paroxysmal cough, ending in a whooping inspiration. Symptoms: Often divided into three stages; first, catarrhal. At this time the symptoms chiefly suggestive of the common cold—slight elevation of fever, sneezing, rhinitis, and dry cough. Irritability and loss of appetite. After 7 to 10 days, the second or paroxyhsmal stage sets in. The cough is more violent and consists of a series of several short coughs, followed by long drawn inspiration, during which the typical whooping is heard, this being occasioned by the spasmodic contraction of the glottis. With the beginning of each paroxysm, patient often assumes a worried expression, sometimes even one of terror. The face becomes cyanosed, eyes injected, veins distended. With the conclusion of the paroxysm, vomitting is common. At this time also, there may be epistaxis, subconjunctival hemorrhages, or hemorrhages in other portions of body. Number of paroxysms in 24 hours may vary from 3 to 4 up to 40 or 50. Following an indefinite period of several weeks, the stage of decline begins. . . .[2]

One of the major breakthroughs in twentieth-century medicine was the development of an effective pertussis vaccine in the mid-1940s. It sent the rate of death and incidence plummeting. The vaccine currently administered in the United States is basically the same as the original version, although intense research is under way to find a better vaccine. While extremely effective in preventing the disease, the vaccine does cause more side effects than other vaccines used in regular "well baby care," including vaccines to prevent polio, mumps, measles, diptheria, and rubella. Minor reactions to pertussis vaccine—fever and irritability—are com-

mon. Severe reactions are rare. The risk of irreversible neurologic damage is only one in 100,000.[3]

The WRC-TV story stated that one in 700 vaccinated children risk serious side effects from the pertussis part of the
vaccine. One in one hundred thousand children, according
to the news account, may suffer neurological problems from
the shots. The story implied a cover-up of problems by pediatricians, the FDA, and the CDC. It featured comments of
parents whose children had suffered harmful reactions to the
vaccine. The TV documentary cited one article in the medical
literature as proof of the incidence of reactions, but it failed to
note the conclusion of the study—that "benefits of pertussis
immunization far outweigh the risks."[4]

The medical news weekly *Medical World News* examined the
story in a June 7, 1982, "Medicine and the Media" column by
writers Lois Wingerson and Mark Bloom.

### Press Report Called "Inexcusable"

The medical establishment reacted strongly to the story.
Dr. William H. Foege, CDC director, charged: "We consider
the program to have been distorted, verging on the irresponsible. Attempts are being made to provoke a major controversy where one does not exist."[5] Dr. Edward A. Mortimer,
Jr., chairman of epidemiology and community health at Case
Western Reserve University and spokesman for the American Association of Pediatrics in the documentary, called the
broadcast a "disaster" because it virtually ignored the hazards of the disease itself. The short segment on the "Today"
show, which reached the larger audience, included scarce
mention of the hazards of whooping cough. The news story,
which emphasized the possibility of brain damage from the
vaccine, failed to point out that brain damage from pertussis
itself (one in eight thousand cases) is much greater.

Lea Thompson, producer of the documentary, defended her work, saying she was careful "not to take a point of view as to the risk of the vaccine versus the risk of the disease. That is up to the medical community. Our objective in doing the story was to put forth enough information in order that parents and doctors could have a dialogue on the vaccine."[6]

While many parents only questioned their pediatricians about the vaccine risks, at least some failed to heed the medical profession's advice that the vaccine was necessary, and they delayed vaccinating their children.

The television portrayal of the hazards of pertussis vaccine illustrates the ephemeral nature of TV journalism. Viewers leave with a perception, based on pictures. Many viewers trust the media and believe the producers wouldn't televise information unless there was a real danger. While concern was justifiable, there was no need for the ensuing panic. An objective account of pertussis would have included pictures of funerals of children in Britain who died during a whooping cough outbreak five years earlier. That outbreak has been linked to similar scare stories in the British press that discouraged DPT shots.

### British Press Blamed for Epidemic

Beginning in 1976, the lay media in Britain began extensive reporting of the side effects of pertussis vaccine. Until that time, 76 to 81 percent of all children two years of age or younger had received full immunization against whooping cough. But after two years of heavy media coverage of the side effects controversy, the level of protection dropped to only 30 percent in 1978 "as a direct consequence of the adverse publicity of potential side effects," says Dr. Vincent A. Fulginiti of the Department of Pediatrics at the University of Arizona.[7]

The drop in immunization was blamed for a whooping cough epidemic. More than one hundred thousand cases (including twenty-eight deaths) were reported from 1977 to 1979, followed by a second epidemic in 1982, when more than sixty-five thousand incidents resulted in fourteen deaths.

The British press—both newspapers and television—dramatized the side effects and gave extensive coverage to critics of vaccination while casting doubt on the veracity of statements from government health officials who encouraged vaccination.

Some journalists lost their objectivity. The *London Times* medical correspondent, Oliver Gillie, inserted his own opinion on the hazards of pertussis vaccine. In a June 13, 1976, article, "Vaccines: What Every Parent Needs to Know," he wrote:

> In view of the serious doubts about the value, the safety, and the original testing of whooping cough vaccine, our considered advice is that parents should not give this vaccine to their children unless they are living in crowded conditions.
>
> But we are bound to say that many doctors will disagree strongly with this advice. If there were to be a serious whooping cough epidemic, then it would, of course, be necessary to consider how this advice should be modified.[8]

Those words proved to be prophetic, as the first whooping cough epidemic began to sweep the country one year later. The article also triggered criticism from doctors who believed in the need for vaccination. London physician Dr. Geoffrey Edsall wrote: "Oliver Gillie's effrontery in offering his 'considered advice' on vaccines indicates that he is suffering from that familiar journalistic ailment: a little knowledge is a dangerous thing."[9]

The *Times* continued to give extensive coverage of the vaccine controversy, including feature stories and photographs of children who suffered brain damage from the vaccine, and comments from physicians who, though in the minority, were quite outspoken in their opposition to immunization programs.[10]

Stories quoting parents opposed to vaccines probably did more to dissuade others from allowing their children to be immunized, such as this account in the April 25 (London) *Times*, titled, "Father Says Vaccine Killed Son":

> A father who blames whooping cough vaccine for the death last May of his son, aged five, told an inquest at Havant yesterday how the boy developed fits as soon as the injection started. Mr. Vernon Hunt said that his son, Jerome, who died at Coldeast Hospital, Fareham, Hampshire, had a fit lasting half an hour after the first and second injections, and after the third his condition worsened. Dr. John Wilson, a consultant at Great Ormond Street Hospital for Sick Children, London, suggested the vaccine theory when he told Mr. Hunt that his son died from brain damage. Dr. Wilson told Mr. Michael Baker, the Southeast Hampshire coroner: "He was suffering from epilepsy and I suspected that this was an adverse reaction to the whooping cough vaccine." But there was no proof. Dr. Keith Mant, the pathologist, said the boy died during an epileptic seizure, "From the post-mortem, it is not possible to establish a link with the vaccine." The jury returned an open verdict.[11]

Stories such as this, which placed the scientist's comments at the end of the article, were weighted in favor of immunization opponents.

By the end of 1982, amid growing concern over the dramatic increase in whooping cough cases, coverage of the side-effects tales tapered off. But a 1983 television program touched off the debate again. The May 6, 1983, newscast prompted Drs. David L. Miller and Euan M. Ross of St. Mary's Hospital in London to complain in the *British Medical Journal:*

> We were sad to see yet another emotionally charged and misinformed television programme on pertussis vaccine, just when one hoped a sense of balance was beginning to return to public perception of this vexed subject. . . . We know of some who were very fright-

ened by what they saw and told us they would never have their children immunized as a result—a sad commentary on the effect the programme produced. We fear the consequences for some children who may remain unprotected against a vicious disease because of this programme.[12]

## Parents Confused by Media Hysteria

Vaccines have dramatically reduced death and illness from many infectious diseases: smallpox has been eradicated worldwide; in the U.S., cases of paralytic polio dropped from 57,000 cases in 1952 to only four in 1984; and, the incidence of measles dropped from nearly 900,000 cases and 2,250 deaths in 1941 to 1,500 cases and only two deaths in 1983. Unfortunately, vaccines carry some risks, occasionally resulting in complications in a small number of children. Nevertheless, medical authorities overwhelmingly agree that the public health balance tilts strongly in favor of vaccination.

Emotion-packed news stories of children who suffer serious side effects fail to give the public an accurate picture of the true danger of vaccinations. In the case of pertussis, some children actually suffered an avoidable disease because their parents were swept up in the media-caused hysteria.

# 16 Pinwheel Surgery Controversy

How does the lay press cover medical controversies? Should disagreements between physicians be aired in the public domain, thus allowing the consumer to decide merits of a procedure before the medical establishment reaches consensus? The following story illustrates the problems that arise when this happens.

The formal medical name for the operation is "radial keratotomy," but thanks to popularization by the lay press, it has become more commonly known as "pinwheel surgery"—a relatively simple thirty-minute operation that seeks to give nearsighted people normal vision. Nearsightedness ("myopia" in medical parlance) is caused by a slight bulging of the cornea, the clear front portion of the eye. In radial keratotomy, a surgeon makes a series of tiny slits arranged like spokes on a wheel that radiate outward from the center of the cornea to its edge. As healing occurs, the natural curve of the eye flattens out, thus reducing the bulge and improving sight.

Beginning in early 1980, newspapers and magazines began carrying stories about this "exciting, new, and controversial" surgery that held out hope for ten million nearsighted Americans. ("Imported Eye Surgery Stirs a Medical Debate," *Detroit News*, March 13, 1980; "A Surgical Cure for the Myopic," *Newsweek*, March 31, 1980; "Surgery That Can Correct Nearsightedness," *Business Week*, September 15, 1980). These and other news stories reported that American physicians were beginning to offer the procedure as a viable alternative to glasses and contacts.

Actually, the surgery was not really new. A Japanese physician, Tutomu Sato, published results in 1953 in the *American Journal of Ophthalmology,* claiming "This new surgical approach to myopia is a proven, safe method, which definitely cures or adequately alleviates over 95 percent of all cases of myopia in Japan."[1] But Sato's patients also had problems; they later developed glaucoma and cataracts, so he stopped operating.

In 1974, a Soviet surgeon modified Sato's operation after seeing a youth with nearsightedness experience improved vision following a freak accident in which he cut his eye with a bottle. The Soviet claimed to have found a way to avoid the post-surgical complications that plagued Sato's patients. Word of the Soviet's success spread to the United States, thanks mainly to a Detroit doctor who observed the operation in the Soviet Union and began performing the surgery in this country in 1978.

While some eye surgeons welcomed the procedure, others were skeptical. The *Harvard Medical School Health Letter* favored "watchful waiting," and reserved judgment until there was more experience with more patients over a longer period of time.[2] The medical debate was heated. It even resulted in lawsuits against the critics by surgeons who favored the operations; they claimed the skeptics were interfering with their medical practice—and income—by raising questions, and steering away patients.

But many eye surgeons were concerned that the procedure might cause infections or long-term damage to the cornea. The American Academy of Ophthalmologists and an advisory council to NIH both issued warnings about the operation, urging restraint in its use.[3] Because of these reservations, the National Eye Institute in 1981 launched a five-year study called "Prospective Evaluation of Radial Keratotomy," or PERK, to evaluate the procedure's safety and effectiveness.

## Medical Debate Downplayed

News stories about the unusual surgery tended to follow the same outline: first, introduce a patient; second, describe the surgery; third, chronicle the strange Soviet-American link; and, finally, mention the medical controversy.

The June 5, 1983, story in the *Columbus* (Ohio) *Evening Dispatch* ("Far Out Surgery for the NEARSIGHTED"), was a typical account of the introduction of radial keratotomy in a community. The story opened this way:

Carl R. Clay Jr. lived in a world of blurred shapes and missing detail. Minutes after a relatively new eye operation, Clay was reading a wall clock across the postoperative recovery room. "I could tell the improvement immediately," Clay said. "It was fantastic." Clay's enthusiasm could easily be shared by millions of Americans who are nearsighted.[4]

The story began on the newspaper's front page, but not until the fourteenth paragraph, inside on the jump page, did the story mention the controversy, noting that some doctors "have greeted the experimental operation with less than Clay's enthusiasm."

Following a similar news story profiling the first patient in Jacksonville, Florida, to undergo the surgery, the Duval County Society of Ophthalmologists became outraged. To counter the positive news account, it paid for a quarter-page advertisement to warn the public about possible side effects. Individual doctors also wrote letters to the editor regarding the procedure. (The patient also wrote her own letter, defending her decision to have the surgery done.)

Here's how a St. Paul newspaper opened a story, titled "Experimental Surgery Raises Hopes for Nearsighted":

Donald Bisel, an avid swimmer, found it quite inconvenient when he couldn't recognize someone standing in a pool a mere 15 to 20 feet from him.

The Burton, Minn., man said he had lost many contact lenses while swimming.

While pursuing another hobby, snowmobiling, Bisel said his glasses would fog up.

And when he took off his glasses, he said he often had trouble seeing them when he was only 10 feet or so from where he had left them.

Now, thanks to a new surgical technique, Bisel requires no correction of vision in one eye, and only minimal correction in the other. He feels he will be able to pass the vision test to drive without glasses or contacts.

After so many years of nearsightedness, "it's like a blind person being able to see," Bisel said, adding that he has been reading more.[5]

In a forty-four-inch story, only one paragraph mentioned side effects!

### Government Study Seeks Objectivity

The PERK study drew extensive news coverage when it began. Both AP and UPI newswire services issued stories in November 1981, announcing that nine eye centers would participate in a $2.4 million federally-funded program to evaluate the procedure. The first PERK report, issued in November 1984, found that the procedure produced favorable short-term results in 435 patients; nearly 80 percent achieved 20/40 vision on standard eye charts, and there were many cases of patients having normal or near-normal vision following the operation. That report drew widespread press coverage (i.e. "Study Backs Controversial Eye Surgery," *St. Paul Pioneer Press*, November 15, 1984).

But eighteen months later, the PERK study began to find that the procedure was less than perfect: a significant number of patients were disappointed in the surgery's long-term effect. In a survey of 355 patients who had undergone the operation, 48 percent said they were very satisfied with the results, 42 percent were moderately satisfied, and 10 percent were very dissatisfied. And while 12 percent said they experienced "a lot of trouble" with fluctuating vision before surgery, 34 percent have reported that problem a year later. Some surgeons began reporting "disasters" with the operation, including the blinding of seven patients.[6] Results of the side effects were reported at the meeting of the American Academy of Opthalmology. This story of possible side effects drew scant media interest.

### 180,000 Americans Undergo Eye Surgery

By 1986, an estimated 180,000 Americans had undergone radial keratotomy. Many were probably encouraged to do so by their ophthalomologists. But undoubtedly some sought treatment because of the nature of the press reports. News stories were mostly upbeat and included comments from patients who had undergone successful surgery.

One of the few publications to treat early results with caution was the *Harvard Medical School Health Letter.* It advised readers in the February 1985 issue:

Only time will tell us whether late side effects will constitute a delayed risk that we don't yet know about. Many distinguished eye physicians are still concerned about the possibility of serious complications, such as late corneal damage, occurring years after the operation. So although the operation has replaced glasses or contact lenses in the large majority of patients over the short haul, our message today remains the same as it was in 1980. Until we know the long-term safety and effectiveness of radial keratotomy, we should be very cautious about it as an alternative to safe and adequate methods of correcting vision.[7]

Later in 1985, articles began appearing in medical journals noting complications of radial keratotomy. Besides minor problems such as fluctuating vision and glare, some patients experienced more serious outcomes, including cataracts, traumatic rupture of the globe, infections, ulcers, and scarring. Although the large majority of people seem to have experienced none of these complications, doctors have been urged to warn patients about the possible serious outcome because its risk-benefit ratio is still being defined.

The question of long-term safety of radial keratotomy remains clouded. Yet a reading of these early newspaper and magazine articles gives the strong impression that it is, indeed, a "miracle surgery" and that complications, if any, are rare and minor. That may, in the long run, be true for the majority of people. But news accounts that tout early successes distort the public's view of research in progress, and make it much more difficult for scientists to produce objective data. Just like pre-trial publicity has been ruled an influence factor before a legal trial, so, too, can publicity affect the public's perception of a medical development.

None of the ten news stories surveyed for this book included any detailed account of the scarring, blurred vision, or blindness that can result from the surgery. The news consumer deserves to be told the whole truth!

# 17 AIDS

No medical story in history has attracted as much press attention as AIDS—the familiar acronym for acquired immune deficiency syndrome. Although AIDS is unquestionably a dreadful disease and has dominated the front pages and television news programs since 1982, we should try to keep AIDS in perspective. More people (mostly children) die of malnourishment than die of AIDS in the world today.

AIDS coverage has tested the abilities of even the best medical reporters, forcing them to ferret out truth from the often contradictory messages emerging from the medical community. Using words like "mysterious," "incurable," and "Andromeda strain" to describe the strange disease, fear-provoking stories have saturated the news media. The ensuing panic, regardless of the real danger of AIDS, was inevitable as the public was barraged with headlines such as: "AIDS: Fatal, Incurable & Spreading," "AIDS: A Spreading Scourge," "AIDS: A Growing Pandemic?" "Rx for AIDS: A Grim Race Against the Clock," and "A Scourge Spreads Panic."

The cover of the August 12, 1985, *Newsweek* blared:

AIDS: It is the nation's worst public-health problem. No one has ever recovered from the disease, and the number of cases is doubling every year. Now fears are growing that the AIDS epidemic may spread beyond gays and other high-risk groups to threaten the population at large.

Who's to blame for the panic? The news media, the scientific community, and the nature of the illness all share responsi-

129

bility. It is not the purpose of this chapter to examine the news media's role in the propagation of fear. (See "AIDS Panic: Who's to Blame" by Judy M. Ismach in *Medical World News*, August 8, 1983). Instead, we shall review how the press has handled the rush to find effective AIDS treatments.

In 1985, the tone of media coverage took a dramatic turn as two experimental drugs—HPA-23 and cyclosporine—emerged as possibly the first effective anti-AIDS medications. (Some press reports overlooked the 1983 hype of interleukin-2 as a possible AIDS treatment.) Both drugs came to the attention of the popular press in unusual circumstances. In both cases, scientists were responsible for raising hopes of AIDS victims prematurely, going public after completing only limited studies and without review and endorsement by other experts, many of whom attacked their French colleagues and the press for sensationalizing the story.

### Educational Seminar Goes Awry

On July 8, 1985, French researchers announced at a New York press conference that the drug HPA-23 appeared to inhibit reproduction of the virus believed to cause AIDS. Tests had been completed on only four patients, but one of them—a fifteen-year-old boy with hemophilia—was doing well more than a year and a half after therapy. (The drug wasn't really new, however. It had been discovered thirteen years earlier to treat Jakob-Creutzfeldt disease, a rare and fatal neurological disorder caused by a virus.)

The HPA-23 announcement came during a symposium sponsored by the Scientists' Institute for Public Information and the AIDS Medical Foundation. The seminar was called to educate the press about the current status of AIDS research in hopes of defusing the sensational news accounts. In discussing HPA-23, Dr. Luc Montagnier of the Pasteur Institute emphasized: "This is not a cure, and we don't know if it will work, but it is certainly worth testing."

Despite the scientist's cautionary comments, the story prompted extensive news media coverage with headlines such as "New Drug Appears to Curb AIDS Virus," in the *New York Times*, "Test of anti-AIDS Drug Successful: Researchers Say," in the *Houston Post*, and "AIDS Victim Improves; Drug Gets More Tests" in the *San Francisco Chronicle*. "NBC Nightly News" called it a "possible breakthrough in the treatment of AIDS." The *Chicago Tribune* included the following editorial-type comment in its news report: "Researchers do not want to raise false hopes about their work, but *this could be the first breakthrough* in the fight against a disease that has reached epidemic proportions. No treatment or vaccine is available."[1]

To desperate AIDS victims in the United States, whose doctors had told them there was no specific anti-AIDS drug, the French announcement was astounding. Many journeyed to Paris in hopes of obtaining HPA-23. "I've received several hundred calls from the U.S. and more than 100 letters. It is very sad because I have to refuse many patients," Dr. Willy Rozenbaum of the La Pitie-Salpetriere Hospital in Paris said in the aftermath of the HPA-23 news announcement. Even before the HPA-23 news reports, the Paris clinic had a month and a half waiting period for patients. Stories about the desperate Americans with AIDS living in Paris had a tone of hope (*Miami Herald:* "France's AIDS Treatment Lending Hope to Victims"; *San Francisco Chronicle:* "AIDS Victims Seeking Help at Paris Clinic").

The flood of American AIDS patients to France prompted some criticisms of the American press by the French scientists. "We have no breakthrough," Montagnier told *Newsweek* magazine.[2] Dr. Jean-Claude Chermann was quoted in the *New York Post* as saying, "In New York [referring to the news conference], we never said this treatment was a cure. We explained that after treatment we couldn't find the virus, but that the virus might come back. We don't pretend to have a miracle."

HPA-23 had almost completely faded from news accounts when in late July 1985 actor Rock Hudson journeyed to Paris for treatment of AIDS. News of the trip surprised millions of people: it was a shock to his fans who discovered that their movie idol was a homosexual. To AIDS sufferers, his sojourn offered new hope that there was a successful therapy at the end of the rainbow—a therapy called HPA-23! Hudson died a few months later.

The educational symposium, intended to better prepare the media for covering AIDS, backfired. Part of the blame lay with scientists going public with only a handful of patients, even before published results in a scientific journal. (The French scientists published a letter in *Lancet* on February 23, 1986, describing the four patients mentioned at the news conferences.) They were naive to think that comments like "this is not a breakthrough" would be enough to quell a story.

Follow-up feature stories about AIDS patients in France may have misled others about the actual worth of the drug because they quoted anguished patients, some of whom gave glowing accounts about the drug's effect. Said one patient: "I hear a lot of negative things about HPA-23, like the severe side effects . . . I've been on the treatment for four months and I'm not having any trouble at all."[3]

As of August 1988, HPA-23 was still considered an investigational drug. Studies in the United States had found it of only marginal use in treating AIDS.

### AIDS Drug Déjà Vu

On October 29, 1985, another group of French scientists

caused a similar media storm by announcing that they had found a different drug effective against AIDS. This time, the hysteria began when the French Ministry of Social Affairs issued a brief announcement stating that physicians had observed "dramatic biological improvements" in an un-named drug. The communiqué did not indicate how many patients had received the drug, nor for how long. But the news release was enough to rally the media to pursue the story. In response to an avalanche of requests for details, three French scientists were forced to hold a news conference to explain details about their findings.

The physicians claimed they had observed a "dramatic" slowing of the progression of AIDS in one of six patients treated with the drug, while another patient had shown a complete halt in the disease's progress after only five days of therapy. The name of the drug was unexpectedly familiar to the press—cyclosporine. The drug was well-known because it had been frequently mentioned in recent years in association with another popular medical story—organ transplan-tion. The drug, a potent suppressant of the immune system, was credited with improving success rates in patients follow-ing kidney, heart, and liver transplants.

The fact that the anti-AIDS drug was an immunosuppres-sant raised numerous questions from both medicine and the press. How could a drug that suppresses the immune system help a patient whose immune defenses are already badly damaged by the AIDS virus? The French scientists said they didn't know for sure; they speculated that the drug somehow stimulated the T-4 cells that are destroyed by the AIDS virus to defend the body.

To some in the medical press, the cyclosporine story must have seemed like déjà vu. Again, the researchers were French scientists. Again, the report was made public before its pub-lication in a scientific journal. And, again, the results were based on very few patients. Nevertheless, journalists rushed to tell the story of another "possible breakthrough" in the fight against AIDS.

Why did the French scientists go public? They said they did so because it was "ethically necessary" to share what might be an important medical finding. But that explanation was attacked by other scientists who charged that the announcement was ill-timed, irresponsible, and falsely lifted the hopes of AIDS victims.

## Medical Evangelism

Sometimes, the press encounters overly optimistic scientists (See "Medical Evangelists," chapter 3) who feel compelled to release their findings in unorthodox ways. By all scientific standards, the studies involving both HPA-23 and cyclosporine were seriously flawed: there were too few patients who had been receiving the drugs for too short a period to draw conclusions, and their findings had not been reviewed.

Some news reports sought to convey the sense of the doubting scientific community, such as an excellent article by David Pearlman in the *San Francisco Chronicle,* ("Experts Discount French Report on New AIDS Drug") following the cyclosporine announcement.[5] Unfortunately, too many news stories failed to include essential disclaimers from the American scientific community. They gave false hope to the thousands of AIDS sufferers, many of whom lost valuable time and money as they chased after an elusive cure. Some died thousands of miles away from friends and family.

# 18 The Charity Campaigns

Should a child's life depend on a parent's skill with the news media? Or, should one child stand a better chance than another to receive life-saving surgery because his father or mother knows how to use the press to wage a charity campaign?

Public appeals for money for life-saving operations such as organ transplants are almost a regular feature in some newspapers and on televison. The stories generally follow the same script: A child with a rare disease may be rescued by a potentially life-saving operation, but the family needs money to pay the hospital bills. Postscript reads: Please help by sending your contribution to Box X.

The pathos-provoking photographs are nearly identical in these stories—a sickly child, forlorn parents, and a concerned physician, speaking in cautious medicalese, stating that, "Yes, there's always a possibility that this will work for young Johnny and will give him a second chance at life."

Controversy adds another element of reader interest to the charity campaign story, especially if an insensitive institution, such as reluctant insurance company or unbudging government bureaucracy, refuses to fund the operation.

The miracles of modern medicine have put some patients in an untenable position. They can benefit from the new medical technology, but at a price. "It comes down to this: if you've got the money, you live. And if you don't have it, you're going to die," says the father of a four-year-old transplant patient.

Anguished parents are willing to go to desperate lengths to save their dying children. They say it is small sacrifice to open their private lives to media intrusion if that is what it takes to get press attention. For media appeals can raise thousands, even tens of thousands of dollars, enough to provide a "second chance at life."

However, the pot of gold is not there for everyone! The success of charity campaigns usually depends upon the number of people reached. A community newspaper that carries the story of a patient in need will, logically, not draw the same public reaction as a story in a large metropolitan daily because the readership is limited to fewer potential contributors. Television exposure has the broadest appeal, evoking greater empathy because of pictures of hurting people.

An astute reporter wrote: "In the game of media roulette, visibility means money. And money means life." But how does a family gain visibility? How does the media decide who gets coverage? Not every charity story makes the 6 P.M. news or the front page of the newspaper. Why have some stories engendered great interest? Why has the plight of some deserving people been ignored? The following two examples provide at least some of the answers.

### $250,000 Raised in Three Days

When the California-based insurance group Kaiser-Permanente refused to cover a bone marrow transplant for Rachel Escalambre, her parents turned to the San Francisco media for help. Within three days, the massive newspaper and television exposure had raised $250,000—more than twice what the hospital required as a downpayment before allowing doctors to proceed with the costly operation.

Rachel suffered from neuroblastoma, a rare nerve cancer.

When she was diagnosed, only the University of Minnesota Hospital performed bone marrow transplants in small children with this condition. Although bone marrow transplants for other types of cancer, such as leukemia, were done regularly, the physicians had only done three for neuroblastoma, one successfully. Therefore, the treatment was considered "experimental."

Yet the risky procedure offered the only long-term chance of life for Rachel. So her parents decided to take the chance. But they needed to first satisfy the hospital's policy for out-of-state residents. Hospital officials required assurance that the $100,000 would be covered.

Rebuked by their insurer, the Escalambres turned to the press for help in raising funds. "Rachel had a competitive edge," writes Lisa Levitt, of the AP. "She was the first dying child whose story received major media attention in the San Francisco area. And she is exceptionally outgoing, with attractive, articulate parents who came across well on television and in photographs."[1]

According to Levitt, the *San Francisco Examiner* carried the Escalambre's banner, assigning reporter Jennifer Foote to the story full-time for nearly two months. She produced more than thirty stories. Two television stations also followed the Escalambre story closely, even flying to Minnesota to record Rachel's admission, operation, and subsequent discharge.

Rachel survived the operation, and was released from the hospital amid great media fanfare. Several news media accompanied the family on the flight back to San Francisco, where more media awaited their return. Unfortunately, Rachel's story had a tragic ending: she died a few months later when the cancer returned.

### Poor, Black, and Unnoticed

Donje McNair, age five, was black, poor, and terribly sick.

His mother was unemployed, unmarried, and living on welfare in a southside Chicago apartment. Donje, who suffered from a fatal liver disease called biliary atresia, was a good candidate for a liver transplant operation. The University of Minnesota Hospital, however, required that it receive a guarantee that the bill would be paid before allowing the surgery to proceed.

The Illinois Public Aid Department, citing the "experimental nature" of liver transplants, chose not to pay for the procedure. In rejecting the request, state officials also pointed out that three other children in the state needed a transplant operation, and that thirty-two thousand people were soon to be cut off basic medical assistance.

Like other parents, Donje's mother turned to the news media for assistance. Donje's story gained widespread attention in the black press, including two front page articles in the weekly black newspaper the *National Leader*, but drew comparatively limited attention in the major Chicago press. Eventually, a total of sixty thousand dollars was raised—not enough to meet the hospital's requirement. "We can't do a transplant story every week," remarked one Chicago editor, whose paper gave only a few inches to Donje's story. He pointed out that Chicago media had been saturated with several transplant stories prior to Donje. In one case, the media helped raise three hundred thousand dollars for a liver transplant operation for a dying girl. The press had lost interest in transplants, and the community's checkbook was running dry.

Even when media attention began to focus on the public policy issues, the "Donje Fund" was never overflowing. And by the time the state of Illinois agreed to pay a portion of the bill, Donje had lapsed into a coma and was no longer a suitable candidate for a transplant. Donje lost out in the "scramble to dip into the public's pocket before it was emptied," one newsman commented.

## Who Pays for "Experimental Surgery"?

In a sense, Rachel and Donje and their families were caught in a medical Catch-22: insurers refuse to cover a new, potentially, life-saving treatment because it is considered experimental, but such treatments will remain experimental until they have been performed enough times—and have a sufficiently high success rate—to become standard therapy.

There was a time when federal research money was readily available for pioneering medical techniques, such as organ transplantation. In recent years, however, actual research dollars have remained relatively constant, requiring academic medical centers to demand money up front before proceeding with the "developing technology." So families have turned to other sources, including the general public via the mass media, to raise money.

The Catch-22 problem is best typified by organ transplantation, a dramatic and expensive technology, that has incited tremendous media interest since the 1960s when surgeons began to record high success rates for kidney transplantation. Since 1972, the federal government has paid for kidney transplantation and kidney dialysis through a special provision in the Medicare law, called the End Stage Renal Disease (ESRD) program. Success in kidneys led to attempts to transplant other organs—the heart, liver, pancreas, and bone marrow. The government has chosen not to fund these procedures because ESRD now costs nearly $8 billion a year to care for only seventy thousand people.

But academic medical centers have continued to perfect heart, liver, and bone marrow transplants. So who pays? Until recently, some hospitals were able to absorb the cost or passed it on indirectly to other patients. A few insurance companies paid, even though the procedure was often not listed in their coverage plans.

A change in reimbursement began in the late 1970s as third-party payers began to demand a closer accounting of how their money was being used. The government, too, wanted an accounting of how funds were spent. Funds from Blue Cross for patient A, who received an appendectomy, would no longer go to patient B down the hall who had a heart transplant.

## Medical Care by Anecdote

Should one family obtain medical care because they're good-looking, middle-class, and articulate—because they are "mediagenic"? Does the press purposely avoid people who are not well-spoken, poor, and not as well versed in politics? Who gets coverage?

"If you have money, or insurance, you get care. If you have the disease of the moment, if you're resourceful enough to get on the 'Today' show, you get care," says Sarah Rosenbaum of the Children's Defense Fund in Washington, D.C. "It's medical care by anecdote."[2]

The amount of press coverage an "appeal story" draws depends partly on the skill and determination of the patient or the patient's family in working with the media. If the story involves a new angle of some kind (e.g., the smallest, the second child in the family), or if social or political issues come into play, or if the patient's time is quickly running out, then the chance of receiving widespread publicity dramatically increases.

Geography and timeliness of the news story are also important factors. For example, one of the first transplant stories to break in the Chicago area was that of Lauren Kalis, seven months old and suffering from a fatal liver disease. Thanks to massive media attention a few days before Christmas, Lauren's parents were able to raise three hundred thousand dollars. But the baby was judged too ill and too small to undergo the procedure, and died a few weeks later. Donje McNair's story came shortly thereafter.

Obviously, journalists are placed in a tough spot. *Chicago Tribune* columnist Joan Beck explained their plight best.

Every columnist, every editor dreads the calls. What do you say to an agonized parent forced by love of a dying child to beg for help to raise money for a liver transplant? How can you stammer and say well, gosh, we did a story like that last week and another one last month and unless you've got a new angle, we probably shouldn't use another one. By the way, how photogenic is your kid? . . . Should a sick baby's chance for life hang on her ability to smile appealing on cue for TV? Or a parent's knack for finding a fresh angle on a story that's been told too often already? Or to persuade a politician to pull a string? And if it's gut-wrenching to beg for money and publicity for a child, how can people do it for themselves when they need the transplant and the contributions?[3]

## A Tragic Scenario

This discussion is not intended to cast aspersions on the families who successfully use the press to raise money for their dying children. The tragedy lies in the media's failure to develop a reasonable method of covering charity cases, and society's inability to equitably allocate limited medical resources. Meanwhile, the children who are not mediagenic are likely to be shunned—both by the press, and the health care system.

What is the impact on the families that must go to the media for help in publicizing their plight? "It's a terrible thing, but it's something you must do. During the time when you should be with your child the most, you must go to the media and beg," said one mother. "But that's a small sacrifice when your child's life is at stake."

Making use of the media is not a uniquely medical phenomenon. Families who suffer losses by fire or natural disaster often turn to the press to publicize their need. The difference has to do with evenly distributing resources that may mean life or death, rather than property. Medical care by roulette or medical care by anecdote is inequitable, haphazard, and unfair.

Allocation of medical resources should have nothing to do with whether a child can convey an appealing image on the TV screen. Allowing journalists to become arbiters of the new medical technology based on their "news sense" is capricious; it skirts the real issue of how health care will be provided. *JAMA* has called media-abetted liver transplants a challenge to the "equity and decency" of medicine.[4]

Although fund-raising for a general cause rather than an individual case will probably never make front page news, it may just help those who need it the most—those without the wherewithal to come up with the downpayment and the possibly life saving operation.

# III How the Press Can Change Your Behavior

This section looks at the role of the news media in behavior modification: the impact of cigarette advertising on news coverage, the link between alcoholism and alcoholic beverage advertising, and the strange relationship between the incidence of suicides and news coverage.

# 19 Media Promotes an "Inebriated Nation"

FACT: 10.6 million Americans are alcohol dependent and 7.3 million more experience some negative consequences of alcohol abuse such as arrest, impairment of health or job performance, or accidents.

FACT: Approximately 40 percent of automobile fatalities are alcohol-related, killing nearly twenty thousand people a year. Alcohol is involved in 35 percent to 50 percent of marital violence and 10 percent of occupational injuries.

FACT: According to the National Institute on Alcohol Abuse and Alcoholism, alcohol-related problems cost our society $117 billion in 1983.

FACT: Alcohol is a threat to your health, resulting in increased morbidity from cirrhosis, cancer, infection, trauma, and gastrointestinal disease.

FACT: Alcohol advertising is rampant in the American press!

The $1-billion-a-year advertising effort is "industry's program for an inebriated nation," charges Michael F. Jacobson, head of the Center for Science in the Public Interest, in Washington, D.C.[1] Since 1972, the consumer group has called for advertising curbs and the use of warning labels on alcoholic beverages like those on cigarette packages.

At present, the federal government is reluctant to impose restrictions on the advertising of alcohol beverages, although there was a time when alcohol advertising was closely monitored. That was before the repeal of Prohibition in 1933. Today, the FTC has no specific regulations that apply to alcohol, and the Bureau of Alcohol, Tobacco and Firearms has guidelines that affect only alcohol producers—not print and electronic media.

However, the move to curtail alcohol advertising has a growing constituency. In 1986, the AMA endorsed the effort.

## Changing Behavior: A Subtle Process

How does advertising change behavior? The "mass media persuasion process" used by advertisers follows one of three learning models: (1) observational learning, in which the ads use human models, such as sports celebrities, whose characteristics of success and beauty are designed to create a desire to imitate; (2) the psychodynamic model, which emphasizes a link between wealth, sex and romance, achievement and success, and the product; and (3) a portrayal of appropriate social norms and drinking behavior.[2]

How successful are advertisers in changing behavior? Despite extensive research by sociologists, the definitive answer remains elusive because of problems in proving cause and effect. However, opponents to alcohol advertising see trends that link increased advertising to more consumption and, indirectly, to more abuse. Research is sparse and fraught with interpretive problems because of the many other social variables involved in alcohol abuse.

Critics argue that the portrayal of athletic prowess, material wealth, prestige, and a fun-filled lifestyle misleadingly translates to the consumer that alcohol consumption is essential if one is to attain an abundant and rewarding life. In their defense, alcoholic beverage manufacturers and advertisers claim that their messages are not intended to increase sales; they contend advertising is intending to provide comparative information that allows the consumer to select from among the many different products available in the marketplace. This rationale is also advanced by cigarette advertisers. Whatever their intention, the alcohol beverage industry believes that promotion pays off, spending an estimated $1.2 billion a year, according to testimony before a 1985 congressional hearing.

### Medical Community Takes Action

Acknowledging problems in research method and analysis, an AMA committee that reviewed the scientific literature "tentatively concluded" that increased levels of alcohol consumption *can* be linked to a greater prevalance of alcohol-related problems.[3] The AMA committee also cited other conclusions, based on available research. They include:

• Alcohol advertising influenced both brand preference (called market share) and the total volume of alcoholic beverage consumption;

• Alcohol advertising contributes to favorable attitudes toward drinking and positive attitudes toward drinkers;

• To a limited degree, alcohol advertising appears to influence problem drinking.

The AMA conclusions are not universally accepted by all scientists in the field. Nevertheless, in its report, contained in the September 19, 1986, issue of *JAMA*, the AMA called for further study to measure the effects of disclaimers in alcohol ads and to determine if educational messages urging moderation or warnings against drinking and driving had any impact.

### Calling for Changes

Despite the controversy over whether a casual link exists between advertising and alcohol abuse, the AMA committee has called for radical changes in how the alcohol beverage industry sells its wares. The AMA approved the following five-point program because it was "deeply concerned over the extent of abuse of alcohol in American society today and the use of alcohol by young people and pregnant women."[4]

• Further research, conducted by impartial and independent agencies, is needed to provide definitive evidence on whether advertising contributes to alcohol abuse. (Some research into the effect of alcohol advertising has received financial support from the alcohol industry, thus leading some authorities to doubt the conclusions of these investigators.)

• Distributors of alcohol beverages should cease advertising directed toward youth, such as promotions on high school and college campuses.

• Advertisers and broadcasters should work together to eliminate television program content that depicts irresponsible use of alcohol without showing its adverse consequences, such as the harm done to a fetus if a woman drinks while she is pregnant, and the broken bodies that result from drunk driving.

• Health education labels with messages focusing on the hazards of alcohol consumption should be used in all alcoholic beverage advertising.

• The AMA as a body should encourage the alcoholic beverage industry to accurately label all product containers, detailing ingredients, preservatives, and ethanol content.

## FTC Asked to Impose Restrictions

In 1985, the Center for Science in the Public Interest, with support from twenty-eight other private organizations concerned with the impact of alcohol on the public, petitioned the FTC to impose restrictions on alcohol beverage advertising.[5] The consumer groups charged that certain alcohol advertising practices were deceptive and unfair because they portrayed alcohol use in an appealing manner. Such promotion information, according to the petition, results in increased consumption and abuse.

In response, the FTC chose not to institute any industry-wide investigation or to launch any enforcement proceedings against advertisers for violating any existing federal statute. Instead, the agency pledged to continue its ongoing review of alcohol advertising.

On a more hopeful note, legislation has been introduced in the U.S. Congress that calls for a study of advertising and promotion of alcohol advertising and for the Surgeon General and FTC to make recommendations for legislation based on the results of that study.

# 20 Tobacco Industry's "Switch to Print" Pays Off

Tobacco causes more death and suffering among adults than any other toxic substance in the environment. Consider these facts:[1]

• Worldwide, 2.5 million people per year die from tobacco's effects.

• More than thirty thousand scientific papers have linked cigarette smoking to diseases, including cancer, heart disease, emphysema, and bronchitis.

• Tobacco kills thirteen times as many Americans as hard drugs do, and eight times as many as automobile accidents.

Besides causing death and suffering to the smoker, cigarettes have secondary effects. Nonsmokers who are exposed to smoking—passive smokers who inhale the smoke from others' cigarettes—have shown a higher incidence of smoking-related diseases, too. Tobacco also endangers the lives of children. The smoking of mothers diminishes both the mental and physical capacities of their offspring. Nicotine passes through the mother's blood and crosses the placenta. In one U.S. study, smokers gave birth to underweight babies twice as often as non-smoking women. Because birth weight is a key factor in infant mortality, tobacco seriously endangers infants' lives.

Since 1964, the medical community, following the now famous Surgeon General's report on the hazards of smoking, has waged a battle to counter the smoking forces. In 1986, the AMA called for a ban on all forms of tobacco advertising.[2]

If smoking is the number one health problem in America today, as the AMA contends, then medical reporters for the lay press should be covering the story as closely as "a tick sticks to a hound," to borrow a time-worn phrase. Not so. Unfortunately, the story of the tobacco link to cancer and other diseases often is either ignored or buried in the back sections of some lay publications, according to several reports by both journalists and public health experts.

Elizabeth M. Whelan, executive director of the American Council on Science and Health (ACSH) and former researcher at the Harvard School of Public Health, has led the attack on the press for failing to tell the cancer-tobacco story. She and her colleagues at ACSH, a private nonprofit group based in New York, contend that cigarette advertisers have influenced the editorial policies of some wide-circulation publications. They have labelled the reluctance of these magazines to tell the cancer story a "conspiracy of silence."[3]

To prove the point, the ACSH analyzed news coverage of cancer-smoking for a twelve-year period (March 1967– February 1979) in twelve women's magazines (*Good Housekeeping, Seventeen, McCall's, Vogue, Harper's Bazaar, Cosmopolitan, Mademoiselle, Redbook, Family Circle, Ms, Ladies Home Journal*, and *Woman's Day*). Results of the study were published in the *Journal of Public Health Policy* in 1981.

The researchers chose this group of magazines because surveys have shown that they are an important source of information for middle and upper class lay people, especially women. In recent years, women are smoking in increasing numbers and, at the same time, are experiencing a rise in cancer incidence rates, as well as in other diseases that have been linked to smoking. These include heart diseases, chronic bronchitis, and emphysema.

Here is a summary of the ACSH findings as reported in the *Journal of Public Health Policy:*

• Of the twelve magazines, *Good Housekeeping* stood out above all as covering the smoking-cancer story in depth. The magazine, which has a policy not to accept tobacco advertising, devoted six major articles to antismoking during the survey period. Of the remaining eleven magazines, however, three carried two antismoking articles during the period while eight carried none. During this era, the researchers noted, new scientific evidence surfaced showing the hazards of smoking to women, particularly expectant mothers.

• ACSH invited editors and publishers of the twelve magazines to participate in an antismoking campaign, to be held in July 1980. ACSH said a similar cooperative effort had been used to focus attention on the Equal Rights Amendment; it had drawn widespread media interest. But only one magazine agreed to carry an article on the hazards of smoking; most publications never responded to the ACSH request.

• "The paucity of reporting on the health effects of smoking in most women's magazines is no accident," the authors concluded. "ACSH members who write health articles for these magazines have been told repeatedly by editors to stay away from the subject of tocacco. Information on the relationship of smoking to health has been edited out of several pieces submitted by ACSH writers."

• The financial dependence of the magazines on tobacco advertising may have had some impact—both direct and indirect—on the editorial policy. The experience of *Mother Jones* magazine was offered as a case in point. After the magazine published an article on smoking in the April 1978 issue, eighteen thousand dollars worth of advertising was immediately withdrawn by a tobacco company. And two weeks after a second article on the dangers of smoking appeared in January

1979, the two remaining tobacco companies cancelled their contracts with the publication.

• Peter N. Georgiades, general counsel for Action on Smoking and Health, was quoted as saying the relationship between editorial policy and advertising represents "the crassest case of journalistic prostitution one will ever see. Many weekly news magazines give only the most washed out, bleached coverage of cigarettes' effect on human health. . . ."

ACSH director Whelan kept up her crusade to expose the press's "silence conspiracy" in a November 1, 1984, editorial in the *Wall Street Journal* in which she told how *Newsweek* and *Time* magazines had edited copy submitted by medical societies to run in special sections on health.[4] The *Newsweek* incident focused on a November 7, 1983, special sixteen-page section on personal health care. The insert, Whelan charged, "virtually ignored the subject of hazards posed by cigarette smoking." In the October 8, 1984, issue of *Time*, a special advertising supplement on "Lifestyle/Healthstyles" was advertised as being written in coordination with the American Academy of Family Physicians. But, according to Whelan, the president of the doctors' group said the strong statements on the risks of cigarette smoking were deleted. He charged, "*Time's* editors blunted, short-circuited and impaired the credibility of [their message] by cutting out all negative references to smoking." A *Time* spokesman denied that the final changes were made without the academy's approval, said Whelan in her editorial.

One of the first analyses of press coverage of smoking was by R.C. Smith in the *Columbia Journalism Review.* His January 1978 article, "The Magazines' Smoking Habit," found that magazines that have accepted growing amounts of cigarette advertising have failed to cover tobacco's health threat.[5]

Here are Smith's findings:

• The most aggressive anti-tobacco news coverage appeared in the *Reader's Digest* and the *New Yorker*, neither of which accepts cigarette advertising. The *Digest*, with a long history of medical articles dealing with the tobacco-disease link, was unique, however, except for the *New Yorker's* articles by reporter Thomas Whiteside on the political and advertising strategies of the tobacco industry.

• Both the women's magazines (with the exception of *Good Housekeeping*) and the men's magazines avoided the subject during the seven years that Smith reviewed the magazine subject matter.

• The "most curious performances" by magazines were those of the nation's two largest news magazines, *Time* and *Newsweek*. While both reported small stories about medical developments on cancer and cigarettes, neither carried a comprehensive article on the subject during Smith's period of observation. He noted that both magazines carry between six to eight pages of cigarette advertisements in each issue.

• "Why," Smith questioned, "have no thorough accounts of the destructive role of cigarettes in our society appeared in American magazines that accept cigarette advertising?" Although some editors may have grown tired of the story, Smith concluded: "But when, over a period of seven years, the hazards of a virtually useless product that happens also to have killed hundreds of thousands of Americans fail to attract the attention of even a single magazine that publishes ads for that product—when this happens, one must conclude that advertising revenue can indeed silence the editors of American magazines."

Interestingly, Smith's article brought no response from any publication in the letter's column. But two letters were printed in response to the story—one from a senior vice president of the Tobacco Institute, a pro-industry group, and one from

Whelan. The institute challenged Smith's analysis, while Whelan offered praise.

## Advertisers Switch to Print

Until 1971, the tobacco industry used television as its primary advertising vehicle. Approximately two-thirds of its advertising budget was spent on TV commercials. But the industry voluntarily agreed to remove ads from the airwaves. Why the switch to print?

The action has been traced to a critical decision made in June 1967 by the Federal Communications Commission (FCC). In response to a petition filed by a consumer activist attorney, the FCC ruled that, under the fairness doctrine, broadcasters were required to make available free air time for antismoking messages. The rationale was simple: because the prosmoking messages were dealing with a controversial issue of public importance, there was a need to tell another side of the story. As a result, thousands of messages warning consumers of health hazards of smoking began appearing on television. The antismoking public service messages never matched cigarette commercials minute-for-minute, but millions of dollars of air time still was given to the antismoking forces free of charge. In 1969, the second year of the antismoking campaign, cigarette sales declined more than 12 billion.[6]

After the tobacco industry agreed to remove its ads from television, the FCC ruled that broadcasters were no longer required to run antismoking messages. The antismoking campaign on television became a voluntary effort, confined mostly to a few "public service" messages that aired at non-prime-time hours.

The tobacco industry didn't stop selling its product to the consumer, however. The millions of dollars spent on televi-

sion commercials were diverted into magazine and newspaper advertising, where there was no government regulation that required "equal space" be given to the antismoking
forces.

A few publications have resisted the financial temptation
to carry cigarette ads. They have placed principle ahead of
profit. Unfortunately, they are few in number (*Reader's Digest,
Good Housekeeping, National Geographic,* the *New Yorker* and
*Consumer Reports* all have banned tobacco ads). In an editorial
on the subject of cigarette advertising, the *New Yorker* wrote:
"The publishers want the money and feel they need the money—and, indeed, for some national publications the annual
revenues from cigarette advertising do make the difference
between profit and loss."[7]

In 1976, at the time of this editorial, the press was giving
extensive coverage to the FDA's proposed ban on saccharin,
but there was very little attention given to the hazards of
tobacco. This fact led the *New Yorker* to attack its own profession, pointing out that saccharin claimed four hundred lives a
year, while tobacco claimed millions.

> We find it significant that the press has been paying very little
> attention to the issue of cigarettes and public health, and that the
> reporting on this subject has become extraordinarily untenacious.
> After all, the issue is not without interest. The effects of cigarette
> smoking on public health are of an absolutely disastrous order. Ciga-
> rette smoking is the direct cause of approximately eighty thousand
> deaths a year in this country from lung cancer alone. . . . Altogether,
> the deaths from cigarette smoking in this country come to about a
> quarter of a million each year—a figure that dwarfs the figures of
> deaths resulting from other catastrophes, natural or man-made,
> which are extensively reported in the press.

## The Press Is a Propagandist

The public must realize that the news media is not its

health guardian. News organizations cannot be trusted to tell the health hazard story fairly because they are the industry's chief propagandist. Many media organizations are swayed by corporate financial gains to the point that news stories are stifled in fear of the wrath of the advertisers

# 21

## Suicides and the "Power of Suggestion"

Billy Williams, an award-winning police and court reporter for the *Atlanta Journal* in the late 1960s, tells the following story about an unsuccessful suicide attempt:

I was working late one night when I got a call from a guy staying in a room in one of the top floors of the Peachtree Center Hotel. The rooms look out over an expansive atrium, with only a waist-high railing between the walkway and the floor below. The caller said he was going to walk out of the room, and jump over the railing to the concrete floor below. But before he jumped, the caller told me he wanted to be sure that a story about his death would appear in the next day's newspaper.

"No story," I told him.

"What do you mean—no story?" the caller demanded. "I'm going to kill myself and it deserves a story."

"People kill themselves all the time, but we don't do stories about it," I countered.

As the caller talked, I told the night editor to pick up the telephone so he could understand what was happening and notify the police of a possible "jumper."

"What if I fall and kill some people in the fall?" the caller wondered.

"No story," I asserted, although an incident such as that would certainly merit a story, probably on the front page of the newspaper.

A few minutes later the police crashed through the door,

and the suicide threat was over. I didn't talk the man out of jumping, but perhaps I did help prevent a potential suicide by keeping him on the line long enough for the police to trace the call and save his life—at least for that night. I was glad I didn't have to write his obituary.[1]

Editors and news directors struggle with the appropriate way of handling suicide stories. Most news organizations have policies that dictate under what circumstances suicidal deaths will be reported. "We have an obligation to report significant events," an ABC News executive has commented, "and yet we have to be sensitive to the possibility of a copycat effect."[2] For a suicide to receive press attention, it must either involve a public figure (such as a politician, movie star, or sports figure), occur in a public place (which will arouse the curiosity of the spectators), or be done in an unusual fashion (such as the suicide of Christine Chubbuck, a television talk show hostess who shot herself while on the air in July 1974).

Despite efforts to minimize news coverage of suicides, such stories do appear. Stories about well-known individuals (the deaths of actor Freddie Prinze, actress Marilyn Monroe, and U.S. Senator John East of Alabama) are unavoidable, news people contend. Yet there are other stories that should either be ignored or downplayed if the press is to perform a public health function. The news media need more people like Billy Williams.

## The Werther Effect

In 1774, German writer Johann Wolfgang von Goethe published a romantic novel, *The Sorrows of Young Werther*, which told the story of a young man who ended his life by shooting himself in the head. As the book gained popularity in Europe, there was an apparent increase in suicides among young people. Blaming Goethe's book for the deaths, authorities in several cities banned it in fear that it would provoke a wave of imitative suicides. This incident led sociologist David P. Phillips to propose the term "Werther effect" to describe the influence of suggestion on suicide.

Phillips, of the University of California at San Diego, has pioneered research into impact of the mass media, specifically newspapers and television, on suicide rates. He has concluded that news coverage of suicides triggers additional suicides as individuals act out imitative behavior. After publishing his ideas for several years primarily in sociological and psychological journals, Phillips's findings were released in the *New England Journal of Medicine* in 1986. In a "Special Article" in the September 11 issue, titled "Clustering of Teenage Suicides after Television News Stories about Suicides," Phillips reported results of his analysis of teenage suicides following thirty-eight nationally televised news or feature stories about suicides between 1973 and 1979.[3] In analyzing more than 12,500 teenage suicides during that period, Phillips and colleague Lundie L. Carstensen found:

• The number of suicides (1,666) following the broadcasts on ABC, NBC, and CBS was 111 more than expected (1,555) based on suicide figures before and after the seven-day period.

• There was a greater increase in suicides proportionate to the number of networks carrying a story. In other words, the more news coverage, the more teenage deaths.

• General information stories about individuals and feature stories about suicides (e.g., "Suicide and the Weather" or "Suicide and the Army") had about the same results.

• No increase in suicides followed fourteen of the thirty-eight broadcasts, while the largest increase (twenty deaths) occurred within a week after back-to-back network reports of the death of actress Jean Seberg and a feature story on teen suicide.

In the same issue of the *Journal,* two researchers from Columbia University reported results of their study of the impact of suicides in television movies. Drs. Madelyn S. Gould of the School of Public Health and psychiatrist David Shaffer analyzed the impact of suicides and attempted suicides in metropolitan New York for a two-week period following four made-for-television movies dealing with suicide that aired between October 1984 and February 1985. Gould and Shaffer found that in every case, both the number of suicides and suicide attempts increased over the comparable period two weeks prior to the broadcast, leading them to conclude that ". . . some teenage suicides are imitative and that alternative explanations for the findings, such as increased referrals to hospitals or increased sensitivity to adolescent suicidal behavior on the part of medical examiners or hospital personnel, are unlikely to account for the increase in attempted and completed suicides."[4]

Critics of the studies pointed out that with a single exception neither study documented that the teen-agers who committed suicide actually had watched television before taking their life. In its defense, the television industry argues that some of the news and feature programming might reap potential public good by increasing public awareness of suicides.

### Press Reports Precipitate the Inevitable?

It has been suggested that press reports are not the cause of the suicide because the event would have been inevitable anyway, and that the press merely precipitated the event. Phillips examined this idea and suggested that, if the reports served as precipitation, then there should be a large decrease in suicides in the weeks after the immediate increase after the news reports, as teenagers moved up their deaths as a result of the publicized death. However, the researchers found instead that the number of teenage suicides remained slightly higher for sixteen days after their eight-day observation period.

Dr. Leon Eisenberg of Harvard Medical School says the suicidal impulse in teenagers commonly waxes and wanes. "If opportunity and means for suicide are not at hand, young persons survive the critical period and their spirits usually spring back," he writes.[5]

Phillips, who grew up in South Africa, has stated that he is strongly opposed to any governmental infringement on a free press. However, he would welcome voluntary efforts to limit or minimize news stories of suicides. He wrote in the *Journal*, "In view of these findings, educators, policy makers, and journalists may wish to consider ways of reducing public exposure to stories, both general and specific, about suicide."

The idea of the press voluntarily curtailing coverage of suicides is not really new. William Farr, considered a pioneer in the field of vital statistics, called for such an action after issuing a report on births, deaths, and marriages in England in 1839–40. Farr, registrar general for the government, urged "by common consent, detailed, dramatic tales of suicide, murder, and bloodshed in the newspapers" because "no fact is better established in science than that suicide (and murder perhaps may be added) is often committed by imitation." He added, "Why should cases of suicide be recorded at length in the public papers, any more than cases of fever."[6]

In 1980, the U.S. Public Health Service set a goal of reducing teenage suicides by 10 percent by the year 1990. Midway through the decade, the rate had remained unchanged. Among U.S. teenagers between fifteen and nineteen years of age, suicide is the second most common cause of death, resulting in almost seventeen hundred deaths a year.

To achieve the suicide reduction goal, experts have called for community-based education and counseling programs and heightened parental awareness to signs of potential suicidal behavior. Parents of suicidal-prone teenagers should become part of this effort. It just might save the life of your son or daughter.

# IV The Media as Voyeur

The word voyeurism is most frequently used in reference to derivation of sexual pleasure by peering into the lives of others. In this section, the term is applied to the behavior of journalists as they seek to use human suffering as a means to derive professional gain for themselves and their employers.

# 22 The Media and Human Suffering

## A Case of Human Suffering: Part I

It's late afternoon on the freeway leading from a major mid-western city. Traffic is at a standstill: the cause is a crash be-tween a moving van and a compact automobile. Police and ambulance crews have snaked their ways through the backup on the freeway and are going about their grim task. As cars pass the scene, they observe the following drama in progress: A bleeding child lies in the grass surrounded by paramedics, police officers, and onlookers. Meanwhile, a rescue crew works frantically to extricate the body of the child's father wrenched between the steering wheel and crushed top of the overturned car. Nearby, a cameraman photographs the ac-tivity as a news reporter graphically describes the condition of the victims and the scene itself. The child is rushed from the scene by ambulance; a second ambulance arrives to re-move the father's body from the mangled automobile. The car is towed away and, one by one, the onlookers, reporter, and cameraman leave. Traffic resumes its normal late afternoon pace. Some of those driving home will arrive in time to watch the evening television news.

## A Case of Human Suffering: Part 2

On the same evening as the crash, a family in the same city is assembled around the television watching the 6 P.M. news. The top news story of the evening is the spectacular crash on the freeway just an hour and a half earlier that left a child in critical condition and killed her father instantly. The on-the-spot color coverage gives the family closeup views of the bleeding child and her mangled father being pried from the car. The reporter accurately describes the suffering of the little girl and the accordian-like appearance of the vehicle. Then, the news program turns to another subject and the family leaves the television to gather for dinner. The scene of the crash has left both the television screen and the minds of the family viewing it in a very few minutes.

In another part of the city, however, the evening news causes an entirely different human reaction. Here, an elderly widow is the viewer. She sees the same reporting of the crash and notes that the remains of the man look remarkably similar to that of her son, her only child. As her fear mounts, she notices the blood-covered jacket that he is wearing—his old high school athletic jacket—and realizes that she is watching her dead son being slowly untangled from his car. She hears the reporter describe the scene, sees her battered granddaughter and is told that her son was crushed to death. The television report never leaves her consciousness. She is haunted by what she saw and heard for the remainder of her life.

Although the vignette described here is fictional, it is representative of what occurs daily in the news media: many people witness the profound suffering and loss of others. For some viewers, the object of their viewing may indeed be a family member or person close to them. The question inherent in such reporting is to what extent should "news" for the majority constitute suffering for the innocent victims of such reporting. Should the news media be allowed to be an agent of voyeurism and vicarious victimization that preys necessarily on those who are unable to defend themselves?

Voyeurism is a word used most frequently to refer to the

act of deriving sexual satisfaction from viewing the intimate aspects of others' lives. Voyeurism in the context of news coverage refers to the derivation of pleasure of viewers and the gain by reporters and news media organizations through observing the intimate—and unfortunate—aspects of others' lives. The scenario described above is an example of such voyeurism. The family viewing the coverage was entertained and relieved, perhaps, to not have been the victims. The newsman had a "hot" story to report—something other stations in the area were not "fortunate" enough to cover. The victims—the child, father, and grandmother—were unknowingly exploited in some of the most intimate aspects of their lives: death, pain, loss of a loved one, and all of the accompanying horror.

Why does this type of victimization happen? The explanation is not simple and involves many parties. The viewer is certainly a necessary component. The human species is innately curious and the ordinary person has a need to know what is going on around him. There is also a need to feel or deny our own fragile mortality. We do this regularly in our lives, through denial, efforts to prolong our lives, and other mechanisms. One of these is through a sort of "mastery" of death by becoming emotionally "immune" to it. Watching death and human suffering on an almost daily basis on television or in the newspaper provides a means for people to become detached, dispassionate, and separated from those experiences. We can watch others dying while we eat our dinners and carry on conversations with family members. Because we normally don't know the victims whom we are watching, it is easy for us to say "better them than me" and turn the channel. The reporting is also dispassionate, which allows us to view horror in a distant, "objective" manner over a very short period of time. And, lest we become too humanly involved, the focus of reporting usually changes within a few minutes to another subject. Most viewers do not "choose" to watch death and suffering; it just comes along as part of the news. The horror stories excite us, perhaps, or make the news carrier seem to be "on the spot" and, therefore, on top of the news. We may even think that the channel has better news coverage because it brings us on-the-scene reporting. Most of these dynamics operate on a fairly subtle, subconscious level. The majority of people would probably choose not to witness human suffering at the expense of innocent victims if they were explicitly aware of the choices they were making and the manner in which such coverage affected them. Part of the issue is pure practicality. If a person got up to switch channels for every eighty-second human suffering story, he or she would seldom have an uninterrupted news program. The same is true for photojournalism in newspapers and magazines.

For the news media, voyeurism means dollars. It means "scooping" other media providers; it means the possibility of winning the continuously escalating competition between news organizations. For reporters, it means advancement, recognition, and the possibility of standing out among others in the field.

But for the victims, news media voyeurism can have lasting and devastating effects. The mental pictures that haunted the widow described above are but one of the potential effects. When a person is photographed and his or her own tragedy is shared indiscriminately with the world around him, the individual is deprived of privacy, dignity, and a sense of control over his life. This is a type of double victimization. The reason that he is the subject of news coverage is because he is already a victim of some circumstance of suffering. This is a requirement to be "newsworthy." Adding the assault of unrequested or unapproved news coverage compounds the suffering and loss of control for the victim. The victim becomes the instrument of pleasure and gain for others and may be left with the psychological damage after the story is made public. One minute of television news coverage, or a photograph in a newspaper or magazine, can leave a lifetime of psychological scars and injury.

So, what can be done about media voyeurism? All parties have a role to play in dealing with the issue. Let's begin with you, the viewer, the news comsumer.

If viewers refuse to tolerate voyeurism by expressing their preferences, changes can occur. You can register a complaint with letters to newspaper editors and television news directors. You might also consider approaching reporters directly with a telephone call to voice your dissatisfaction. And, of course, you can simply stop viewing a particular television channel and avoid newspapers that continually practice media voyeurism. Consumer preference can be a major force in shaping news coverage, but consumers must express their choices.

The role of the news media in dealing with the issue of voyeurism is, obviously, quite complicated. Many news media organizations are responsible and show restraint in the victimization of individuals. In a democracy where press freedom is a fundamental tenet, it's essential that the news media regulate itself relative to this issue. The journalism profession must become more aggressive in maintaining high standards of quality. Without professional standards, the only motivation for the news media as a business will be profit. Journalists must insist on adherence to standards by their colleagues and employers. The victimization of innocent people cannot be avoided unless journalists play a primary role in determining the appropriate approach and limits of their journalistic efforts.

Finally, victims can play a role in curtailing media voyeurism in one of three ways: by preventing news coverage, by limiting the impact of coverage, and, finally, by recovering losses when victimized. The message here is not one of "blaming the victim." It is not our view that victims are responsible for what happens when the news media intrudes upon their lives. Rather, victims must assert as much control as possible in situations in which they are exploited by the news media.

The first strategy is prevention. Although most of us are unable to predict when we may be victimized by the news media, we can become active in our consumer role and state our objections to the victimization of unfortunate people by news people. The second strategy, similarly limited, is for the victim to try and take command of the situation. Don't hesitate to say "no" to unwanted photographs, interviews, or any other type of media intrusion into your life. Assert your right to privacy. What may seem like a harmless interview or photograph may become a major problem to you at a later date for various reasons: there may be potential psychological damage, or you could face possible legal problems that were not fully evident at the time of the interview because you may not have been in full control of your emotional or intellectual facilities. For example, if you are recounting the details of an accident just after it happened, you may not be able to do so accurately because of the emotional intensity of the moment, yet your observation may affect the outcome of legal proceedings at a later date.

Finally, victims can fight back when victimized by the news media. Individuals have certain rights of privacy and control of their own lives. When these rights are violated, our society provides means of seeking redress. There are both legal and nonlegal options open. To determine the legal avenues available, consult an attorney, a legal information service, or library. You may also pursue your grievance by approaching the news organization directly. File a complaint with the news organization's management if you feel a reporter or photographer's conduct was inappropriate, unprofessional, or offensive. Some states have news councils to hear complaints against the media.

Media voyeurism is not an essential ingredient of journalism; in fact, it is not good journalism at all. The pressures of society for sensationalism in reporting, the stiff competition between media organizations, and ambitious reporting all contribute to this unnecessary and frequent victimization of suffering people. Through conscious involvement of all parties, media voyeurism can be dealt with—and eliminated.

# 23 A Patient's Right to Privacy

The following three incidents, which occurred at University of Minnesota Hospital when the author (RCH) was head of the institution's media relations office, illustrate how media voyeurism affects patients and their families who become "newsworthy" because of a medical condition.

## Near Drowning Means Possible Brain Damage

The young couple from rural Minnesota is physically and emotionally exhausted as they wait anxiously outside the pediatric intensive care unit. Inside the glass-enclosed ward, their two-year-old son Jimmy, connected to a respirator, struggles for life following a near drowning.

It had been forty-eight hours since the child's accident and his parents had yet to eat or sleep. Finally, a nurse convinces them to leave the ward to get some breakfast. En route to the hospital cafeteria, they pick up the morning newspaper to catch up on current events as they eat. While awaiting their meal, they run across a three-paragraph story about their son's accident. Without attribution, the story states that if the boy survives, he has a "fifty-fifty chance of permanent brain damage." The parents' grief intensifies.

For the next three days—until the boy's death—reporters make daily calls to the hospital to find out the health status of the child.

A patient's right to privacy may be diminished because he

or she has become involved in a "police case," meaning that a crime or accident has occurred. The press has greater access to information in these situations. Thus, without warning, a family will find that their child's medical condition is "public information" because of the nature of the accident. They may be hounded at the hospital and at home by reporters seeking details about the incident and their reaction to it.

## Please Wait Until Morning

The hospital lobby is filled with reporters who have learned that surgeons are performing a transplant operation on a ten-month-old boy. If he survives, he will be one of the youngest patients ever to successfully undergo the surgery. But the little boy dies on the operating table. His parents, who were courting press coverage a few hours earlier, are in shock. The family sends word to the reporters, requesting that they wait until the next day to announce the death of their little boy—they need time to compose themselves before notifying their friends and relatives about their loss. But the electronic media is unwilling to wait until the morning news broadcast to report the event.

Does the press right to know override a parent's right to grieve? Should the press withhold medical details to protect feelings? "It's not our job to withhold the news to spare feelings," said a reporter who was involved in this incident. "The parents had an obligation to inform relatives promptly, despite their pain."

For some individuals, that is easier said than done. Lay people do not know the mechanics of journalism—such as deadlines and the forces of competition. Their innocence and ignorance can lead to disappointment and heartache.

Families who turn to the media to raise money (See chapter 18, "Charity Campaigns") find that they must make a commitment of time and emotion to satisfy the media's thirst for information. For them, the loss of privacy is a small sacrifice if the press is able to generate money needed to save a loved one's life.

## Checkbook Journalism

A man arrives at the hospital information desk carrying a five-foot stuffed bear. He tells the receptionist that he is delivering the toy to the little girl who, a few days before, had undergone heart transplant surgery. He claims that he is doing so on orders of the chief of surgery. The man is directed to the appropriate nursing ward, where he asks an orderly to direct him to the room of the little girl. Once inside the room, he identifies himself as a news photographer for a national newspaper that is willing to pay the family money in return for exclusive pictures of their daughter.

Individuals who undergo the first-of-a-kind surgery or who are the first to recover thanks to the latest medical gizmo will be pressed by the news media to reveal details about the experience. Some reporters go to great lengths to discover the identity of the patient, even when the family has requested confidentiality. The patient may be forced to decide, as in the case of the little heart transplant girl, whether or not to "sell their story."

Most news media are repulsed by "checkbook journalism," which is routinely practiced by the supermarket tabloids and some European news media. In this case, the chief of surgery had never given permission to deliver the stuffed animal; it was a guise to find the little girl whose name had not been made public.

# V How to Find the Truth

How does the consumer decipher medical news and advertising claims in the press? This section offers a guide through the medical information maze and gives you some hints on how to use a medical library. The second chapter gives you several pointers on how to identify medical quackery, and what can be done to eliminate it.

# 24 A Consumer's Guide to Medical News and Advertising

Consumers should not expect the news media to curtail coverage of medical news and advertising. In all likelihood, the amount of newspaper space and television air time devoted to medicine and health will increase in years ahead. So how does the news consumer decipher fact from fiction in this barrage of information? This chapter seeks to provide you with a guidebook to discovering the truth for yourself.

## Be Skeptical, Cautious, Suspicious

Here's a brief ten-point outline designed to help you interpret medical information in the popular press:

1. When reading or viewing medical news and ads, the cardinal rule is, be eternally skeptical. If something sounds too good to be true, it probably is. Doubt the reporter, doubt the physician, scientist, or patient making miraculous claims, and doubt yourself. By starting from this posture of skepticism, your hopes will not soar to unrealistic heights, only to be dashed later as more evidence comes forth. Why doubt yourself? Because you may have blocked out information, or misinterpreted what was there, because your expectations were unrealistic to begin with.

2. Never believe a news story or advertising promotion that has a single source, especially one of those so-called "experts" who has no affiliation with a reputable medical school or medical research center. Reporters who quote only one informant, or informants from the same corporation or hos-

pital, have not done their job, and the information is therefore suspect.

3. Look for follow-up articles in other news media about the initial medical claim. It's easy to dupe one reporter, especially journalists without a medical reporting background. But it's unlikely that unfounded claims will be hailed by everyone. Look for follow-up articles in medical news magazines such as *Medical World News, Science News,* the *JAMA* news section, the *Medical Tribune,* or the medical and science sections of the *Washington Post* or *New York Times.*

4. Scan the letters-to-the-editor section of both general circulation publications and the scientific journals for the reaction of other scientists to the medical news "breakthrough." Although the publication delay is sometimes lengthy, they are a valuable resource for consumers who want to learn if the medical world is in agreement or contesting a new medical development. Sometimes, these letters comment about media coverage of medicine.

5. Beware of the hornblowers—the PR people—whose identities are masked by titles such as public affairs director, information officer, communications coordinator, or science writer. Remember, PR is a game in which reality is shaped to accent the positive and downplay (or ignore) the negative.

6. Always ask, "Who's profiting?" Any story or advertisment heralding a new hospital technology, a pharmaceutical company's potent pill, or a doctor's unique speciality clinic has an economic angle. A university doctor, who once sought the aid of the public relations office at a Minneapolis hospital remarked, "I'm going public with this clinic for two reasons: first, to help some patients and, second, to make me a lot of money."

7. Watch for criticisms of medical stories. Some newspapers have ombudsmen or reader's representatives to investigate inaccurate or shoddy reporting. Even some magazines

and the electronic media now have in-house watchdogs. If you wonder about a story, try contacting them to see if they can clarify the background of the story.

8. Don't rely on your memory. If you heard a story about a new medical breakthrough on radio or television, forget it and look for another source. TV and radio newscasts function primarily as a headline service—the whole story packaged in two minutes or less. The consumer cannot recall the subtleties; there are none in this format. Unless you have your video cassette recorder tuned in, you can't go back and re-view the report.

9. Contact a third-party for another view of the news story or advertisment. Start with your physician, but if he or she is too busy, or unaware of the story's content, try a foundation, professional organization, or government agency. For example, if the item deals with cancer, see what the American Cancer Society has to say about the work.

10. Find out for yourself. Go to a medical library and begin sleuthing. The next section will tell you how.

### How to Use a Medical Library

You have every right to use a medical library in a state-supported institution. Your best ally in the search for reliable information is the librarian. Explain your purpose and ask for help in locating articles. There was a time when medical librarians were reluctant to assist people in tracking down information, but the courts have ruled that such assistance is not the same as giving out medical advice.

You will probably be directed to one of several indices: *Index Medicus* or *Hospital Index*. They list articles published both in U.S. medical journals as well as those from around the world. The journals include two listings—one by author and another by subject and title.

If you are looking for a general overview article or the current state-of-the-art in treatment, then ask for help in locating *Current Therapy,* an annual review of major diseases and how to treat them. If you are wondering about the credentials of a scientist, check him or her out by reading *Who's Who in Medicine.*

Most biomedical libraries affiliated with medical schools have search services available to provide a computer-produced bibliography—a list of recently published articles or abstracts according to subject, author, or title. The search service is able to tap into MEDLINE, a database of all medical literature, provided by the National Library of Medicine in Washington, D.C. The cost of these searches may vary, but at the University of Minnesota, for example, for fifteen dollars, you can get short abstracts on one hundred recent articles.

## How to Read a Medical Journal Article

Can a layperson unfamiliar with medical terms read and understand original research published in a scientific journal? The answer is a qualified yes, provided you are willing to put forth time and effort. Remember that most news reporters have a general liberal arts background—a journalism degree or a social science speciality. Their only advantage over the layperson may possibly be access to the journal's author, though many news stories are written without the cooperation of the scientist. The information comes directly from the journal article or meeting abstract.

Before reading a scientific article, you must be equipped with two dictionaries—a good standard word dictionary and a medical dictionary. A copy of the *Merck Manual,* which includes profiles of drugs (their actions and side effects), and the *Physician's Desk Reference* (PDR) are also helpful. Introductory textbooks used by first-year medical students are also helpful in putting a subject into context.

Journal articles are organized in the following manner:

*Abstract*—A brief summary, usually not more than one hundred to two hundred words, that precedes the actual article and includes highlights of its methods, results, and conclusion. The key sentence is usually the last one.

*Introduction*—Here you will find the historical framework for the study, including citations of previous work in the same field of study and a statement of purpose: the reason for doing the study.

*Methods and Materials*—This section explains how the study was performed, what drugs were used, and how responses were evaluated. It will also answer questions such as: How were patients recruited? What did they have in common? Was the study placebo-controlled, meaning that one group received a drug and another an inert substance?

*Results*—In this section, the author explains the reactions to the drug or procedure. How many patients improved? Were there side effects? What did the laboratory tests reveal?

*Discussion*—If the study's results run counter to previous reports, this must be explained. New information must be analyzed and put into a context of applicability. This section will state if further studies are needed to answer unresolved questions or problems. Although the final section of the journal article, it is often the first read and includes the most important information.

*Acknowledgments*—On first glance, this may seem like the place where the author only says thanks to colleagues, but you can learn here if the study was underwritten by a medical manufacturer, in which case the article should be looked at with suspicion.

*References*—Supporting documentation can give you some insight into the verifiability of the report. Where were these articles published? Did the author of the article cite his own previous work to justify the present study?

Although the journal article will include the language of science and detailed tables of statistical analysis, you will find that many phrases, especially in the discussion section, are understandable if you read them closely and cautiously.

## How Science Works

The development of a new drug or medical device in the United States involves a long and complex process that can begin in many places—a manufacturer's laboratory, the NIH, or at a hospital or medical research center—but requires step-by-step monitoring before it is made available to the American public. The following, adapted from an article in the *FDA Consumer*[1] will give you insight into the process.

The road to approval of a new therapeutic drug begins with research into the chemistry or anatomy of a disease. The scientist's observation that a certain chemical alters the disease state *in vitro* leads to screening tests in animals to determine if the chemical will produce desired drug effects. If screening reveals a desirable reaction, then additional tests must be done to determine a safe dosage range for humans.

The FDA requires that sufficient animal tests be performed to show that a drug is reasonably safe before trying it on humans. Though the FDA does not monitor animal tests directly, it requires extensive documentation before allowing human tests to proceed. Based on this information, the manufacturer or inventor will be allowed to apply for an Investigational New Drug (IND), status. Granting of an IND means the developer may begin testing in humans.

The first step of human testing, called Phase I, determines a drug's chemical action: how it is absorbed into the body, the safe dosage range, and what is the optimal way it should be given (by mouth in a capsule form or by vein through an intravenous injection). These tests usually involve a small number of patients, usually fewer than ten, who volunteer for the study after being told the possible negative effects of the drug. Initial tests will begin with doses one-tenth or less of what might be expected to be used to actually treat the disease. The dosage is then gradually increased as scientists monitor for possible adverse side effects.

If Phase I tests show the chemical is safe and does produce a sought-after reaction in the body, the drug sponsor may proceed to Phase II studies. These involve human testing on a limited number of patients for the actual treatment of the disease. In this step, investigators again watch closely for side effects and whether there is any impact on the disease process.

The only way to verify that a drug has a healing effect, and the patient's response is not the result of a psychological effect, is to conduct extensive "placebo-controlled randomized" trials. In this way, the true effect of the drug can be determined by screening out other variables, such as the patient's hope for success. The tests may be double-blind, meaning that neither the patient nor the doctors and nurses who administer the drug know who is receiving a placebo and who is being given the active substances. Materials are given code numbers, and a confidential list of allocations is kept by a responsible third party until the study ends, or in case the study is stopped because of adverse reactions. This type of trial may require several years, but it is the only way to differentiate between actual drug effect and placebo response.

If a drug passes all three trials, the sponsor may apply to the FDA for a New Drug Application (NDA). Here, results of the studies will be examined by a variety of experts, including physicians, pharmacists, and chemists. They will examine the benefit-risk ratio of the drug to determine that expected benefits outweigh the side effects. They consider how much risk the public is willing to accept in order to obtain possible benefits from a new drug. No drug is completely free of all risk.

Once an NDA is granted, the manufacturer is required to keep extensive records on production methods, safety, and effectiveness. During the first year of approval, a report must be filed every three months. In the second year, a report is filed every six months, and yearly in following years. If a drug causes unusual or severely adverse reactions at any time, a report must be filed immediately.

# 25 What to Do About Quackery

Many people believe that medical ads are screened by a government agency. This is *not* the case with most health-care products, except for drugs and medical devices that require approval by the FDA. There is no federal, state, or local government agency that approves or verifies claims in advertisments *before* they are printed and aired in the news media. Law enforcement agencies can take action only after the advertisments have been published.

Government efforts to abolish misleading and quack advertising have been woefully lacking, according to a congressional investigation.[1] The problems are many: loopholes in the laws, lack of enforcement personnel, and the extensive amount of time and effort required to investigate and prosecute fraud on a case-by-case basis. Meanwhile, the news media continue to carry quack advertisements for treatments for arthritis and cancer, and fraudulent remedies for baldness, weight loss, and other maladies.

Therefore, consumers must be prepared to resist the quack's lure. That's not always easy because quack products may be based on some medical report that you've heard about in the news. As a general rule, watch out for ads that seem to promise too much too easily. The following tips may help you identify fraudulent advertising, either in mail-order ads or news stories:

• Look for certain red-flag words such as "startling discovery," "cure," "breakthrough," and "miracle." Reputable scientists don't use these terms.

• Doubt any claim for broad application to a variety of maladies, such as snake venom for arthritis *and* multiple sclerosis.

• Beware of testimonials that sound too good to be true. They are! The use of accounts from people who claim they have been healed is not the same as "proof." In many illnesses, a patient responds on his or her own as the body fights off a disease using its own arsenal of immunological and disease-fighting mechanisms. In other cases, the placebo effect may be responsible for improvement. Finally, the patient may still be suffering, but in a period of remission.

• Be careful of claims that the scientist/promoter is a "maverick" who is ostracized by the medical establishment. There is usually a good reason why certain individuals are held in disfavor by the medical community. Also, any claim that the discovery had been overlooked or ignored by the medical community is a signal of fraud.

• Watch for references to "published research." If the article or ad fails to cite the journal, date of publication, and authors, then the article probably doesn't exist. If the huckster does produce a piece of paper that appears to look like it was published somewhere, find out what journal. If the journal is not listed in *Index Medicus*, then it was not peer-reviewed, meaning the article did not go through orthodox channels of scientific evaluation.

• Be careful of claims stating that because a substance is "all natural" or containing only minerals and vitamins that it cannot harm you. This is untrue. Some vitamins and minerals when used in large amounts in conjunction with medications can be harmful, even fatal, as in the case of selenium (See chapter 8).

• Check with the information office of the FDA, either in

Washington or one of its regional bureaus if you have questions about the effectiveness of a new drug.
• Check with a physician or nurse practitioner before buying into mail-order medical products and devices.

## What the Government Can Do

Both state and federal agencies must become more aggressive in policing medical advertising. You, as a consumer, should lobby your elected officials to take up the fight.

The state governments have authority over criminal penalties; they should impose stiffer penalities against fraudulent health ads. According to the congressional report, two-thirds of states have inadequate laws to protect consumers from health quacks.

At the federal level, the U.S. Postal Service, which has an active unit assigned to policing mail fraud, needs more enforcement authority; it cannot, at the present time, obtain the records of health promoters, which makes prosecution difficult. And the FTC must act to stop deceptive advertising.

Congressman Claude Pepper's committee urged federal agencies to form an Anti-Quackery Task Force to develop a concerted plan to attack, investigate, expose, and prosecute health hucksters.[2] Another suggestion was for the Department of Health and Human Services to convene a Congress on Quackery with representatives of both the private and public sectors.

Finally, the government must increase funding of educational efforts that promote accurate information of medicine and health. Public awareness is the strongest defense against health fraud.

# APPENDIX I Publications

*FDA Consumer.* Superintendent of Documents, Government Printing Office, Washington, DC 20402.

Published ten times a year, the magazine is the official publication of the federal Food and Drug Administration, but its articles are well-balanced and listed in the *Reader's Guide to Periodical Literature*. Articles focus on recent FDA decisions on medical products and substances, and investigations into health fraud that come under the jurisdiction of the agency.

*Harvard Medical School Health Letter.* Department of Continuing Education of Harvard Medical School, 79 Garden Street, Cambridge, MA 02138.

The monthly newsletter has been published since the mid-1970s in easy-to-understand language. Articles focus on state-of-the-art treatments, explaining new breakthroughs, and debunking medical myths. Each issue includes a "Medical Forum" article by an expert in a subspecialty who explains the current therapy of a particular disease.

*Health & Nutrition.* Columbia University, New York, NY 10027.

The faculty of Columbia University's School of Public Health and Institute of Human Nutrition publish the monthly newsletter whose purpose is "not to snow you with scientific facts" but to put health in a general context of living well. Past issues have carried articles on contact lenses, fertility drugs, and Alzheimer's disease.

**191**

*Mayo Clinic Health Letter.* Mayo Clinic, 200 First Street, SW, Rochester, MN 55905.

The monthly newsletter by the world-reknowned Mayo Clinic covers current topics in medicine, including new drugs and therapies, as well as ethical issues such as the Baby Jane Doe controversy. Written in layman's language, the newsletter promises to include "health news you know you can trust."

*The National Council Against Health Fraud Resource Center,* Trinity Lutheran Hospital, 3030 Baltimore Avenue, Kansas City, MO 64108.

Publishes newsletter with articles debunking quack remedies. The center also makes available videotapes and lists of medical experts. The council sponsors educational seminars aimed at improving communication between medical people and the news media.

*News and Features from NIH.* Editorial Operations Branch, The National Institutes of Health, NIH Building 31, Room 2B-03, Bethesda, MD 20205.

This quarterly publication includes both in-depth feature articles and short news briefs about recent research developments. Special issues have focused on pain, arthritis, cancer, and other diseases.

*NIH Record.* Editorial Operations Branch, The National Institutes of Health, NIH Building 31, Room 2B-03, Bethesda, MD 20205.

The Record is the internal communication tool for NIH employees. It contains news of new appointments and programs, but often highlights recent medical successes and background information on important research.

*Pediatrics for Parents: The Monthly Newsletter for Caring Parents.* Pediatrics for Parents, Inc., 176 Mt. Hope Avenue, Bangor, ME 04401.

This easy-to-read monthly newsletter focuses primarily on preventive health—the need for fluoridation, dangerous toys—but also includes valuable advice on what to do in the event of medical emergencies in the home.

*Research Resources Reporter.* NIH Division of Research Resources Information Center, Building 31, Room 5B10, Bethesda, MD 20892.

Published monthly by the Division of Research Resources, NIH, the newsletter is for an educated lay audience, but differs from journal articles in that it includes background, quotes from investigators, and a "state of the art" presentation.

*University of California, Berkeley, Wellness Letter.* P.O. Box 10922, Des Moines, IA 50340.

Published monthly in association with the School of Public Health at the University of California at Berkeley, the newsletter features recent and accurate information on nutrition, fitness, and stress management. The eight-page newsletter includes different columns on health myths, ask the experts, and book reviews.

# Medical Information Hotlines and Clearinghouses

**AIDS**—Public Health Service, AIDS Information Hotline, 1-800-221-7044.

**Alcohol**—National Clearinghouse for Alcohol Information, Box 2345, Rockville, MD 20852. 301-468-2600.

**Alzheimer's Disease**—Alzheimer's Disease and Related Disorders Association, 1-800-621-0379; in Illinois, 1-800-572-6037.

**Arthritis**—Arthritis Information Clearinghouse, Box 9782, Arlington, VA 22209. 703-558-8250.

**Blind and Physically Handicapped**—National Library Service for the Blind and Physically Handicapped, Library of Congress, Washington, DC 20542. 1-800-424-8567.

**Cancer**—Cancer Information Clearinghouse, National Cancer Institute, Office of Cancer Communications, Building 31, Room 10A-18, 9000 Rockville Pike, Bethesda, MD 20205.

**Diabetes**—National Diabetes Information Clearinghouse, Box NDIC, Bethesda, MD 20205. 301-468-2162.

**Drugs**—Food and Drug Administration, Office of Consumer Affairs, 5600 Fishers Lane (HFE-88), Rockville, MD 20857. 301-443-3170.

**Health Information**—National Health Information Clearinghouse, Box 1133, Washington, DC 20013-1133. 1-800-336-4797; in Virginia 1-703-522-2590.

**Heart Disease**—Association of Heart Patients, 1-800-241-6993; in Georgia, 1-404-523-0826.

**Kidney Disease**—American Kidney Fund, 1-800-638-8299; in Maryland, 1-800-492-8361.

**Surgical Opinions**—National Second Surgical Opinion Program, Health Care Financing Administration, HHSN 330 Independence Avenue, SW, Room 4231, Washington, DC 20201. 1-800-638-6833.

# APPENDIX **III** A Reporter's Notebook

Victor Cohn of the *Washington Post* has spent nearly four decades communicating medical news to the public. He has excelled as a reporter, author, and lecturer. In the process, he has gained the respect of both fellow journalists and the medical community. From his perspective, journalists and scientists share equal responsibility for miscommunication. While reporters may miss the nuances of a medical development and fail to include caveats, scientists are guilty of overextending the implications of their findings. Thus, Cohn suggests, medical journalists need to be more skeptical when reporting medicine, and more cautious in composing their stories. Says Cohn: "Medical reporters are better educated and more responsible today, but there are still a lot of bad reports, especially by reporters who must dart in and out of a subject, something a sports editor would not tolerate from his staff."[1]

## Prescription for Success

What can the news media do to improve medical news coverage?

1. Reporters should background themselves on a subject before interviewing the physician or scientist. If you plan a career as a medical communicator, get a degree in one of the biological sciences or work in a hospital or research setting to gain an insider's perspective on how medical research is performed.

2. Employ a readback policy. While such an idea is tantamount to heresy in the newsroom, some reporters already do it to guarantee accuracy in complex subjects. A reporter who reads back complicated phrases isn't submitting to censorship. The reporter is simply being responsible—to the source and to the public.

3. Be suspicious. Some scientists choose to proclaim their work to the world via the news media for reasons that aren't entirely altruistic (the medical evangelist). Avoid quoting a single source or representatives from a single institution.

4. Check out the qualifications of people who claim to be "experts." Request from them citations of their publications, then verify them in *Index Medicus*. The library work might delay your story, but it is certainly worth the time and effort to insure accuracy.

5. Develop a network of experts willing to background you on the significance of medical advances. Your pool of confidantes will grow as you establish a reputation as a responsible journalist.

6. Curtail coverage of medical meetings. Use the professional gathering of scientists as a source of background material for future stories.

7. Consider the caveats and exceptions a high priority in a medical news story, even when the extra verbiage makes the story long and cumbersome. If a story based on preliminary research does run, suggest to your editors that it be placed in a back section or page of the paper, or just make a brief mention of it on television.

8. Reporters must have courage to kill a story. This may be difficult when editors insist that a story about cancer or heart disease will be widely read.

9. Editors should not allow neophyte reporters to cover new medical discoveries. Many of the errors in the medical communication process are committed by reporters who don't specialize in medicine but happen to receive a story assignment because the regular beat reporter was either busy or not available.

10. Beware of misleading headlines because that may be the only thing the reader remembers about the story. Don't allow the copy editor to extend the study's implications in order to attract attention.

11. Bring back the National News Council. One of the major frustrations physicians and scientists have with the media is the lack of recourse it offers for correcting errors. While editors and

news directors offer complainants an opportunity to write letters, there is no vehicle on the national level to adjudge issues of interpretation.

## The Need for a National News Council

In 1973, when the press was under attack by the Nixon administration, a group of journalists and interested laymen decided to blunt press criticism by organizing the National News Council. The council's mission was to investigate and judge specific complaints against the news media.

After a decade of limited success, the council disbanded in April 1984. The council was hampered from the inception by a lack of cooperation from major news organizations. Some media refused to participate, fearing that lawsuits might result from council actions finding faulty media coverage. Others believed the council might lead to curbs on First Amendment freedom.

Why won't the press cooperate with impartial bodies? Professor David Cassady, an assistant professor at Pacific University, has suggested there are two reasons for noncompliance: fear and elitism. "Both are unfounded but they still exist," he writes. "Somewhere journalists have associated the absolute protection from legal sanctions provided by the First Amendment with a similar absolutism about their abilities."[2]

# APPENDIX **IV** Rx for Medical People

In 1906, Dr. William Osler, a professor of medicine at England's Oxford University and a pioneer in the study of blood disorders, wrote: "In the life of every physician there comes the temptation to toy with the Delilah of the press—daily and otherwise. There are times when she may be courted with satisfaction but beware! Sooner or later she is sure to play the harlot and has left many a man short of his strength, viz., and confidence of his professional brethren."[1]

Despite Osler's warning, meetings between health practitioners and the lay press often are unavoidable. For a scientist who publishes in a medical journal, refusal to deal with the press means running the risk of the reporter misinterpreting the work and exaggerating its conclusions. Non-academic physicians also can be drawn into the media milieu unexpectedly if their patient is a prominent public individual, or if the family faces serious financial problems that force a public appeal for help. So how should a physician, scientist, or other health professional react when a reporter calls?

1. Request an in-person interview with the reporter. A study by Phillip J. Tichenor of the University of Minnesota School of Journalism and colleagues found that stories resulting from telephone interviews are regarded as less accurate by sources than those resulting from face-to-face questioning.[2]

2. Obviously, choose your words carefully. If you have time, prepare a written statement using language that is comprehensible to a lay person, though still scientifically accurate. Follow the journalist's style of the "inverted pyramid," meaning that the most important thoughts are placed at the top of the article. Some scientists have difficulty talking in "layman's language," in the belief that it somehow diminishes the quality of their work.

3. Request the reporter read his story to you prior to its publication. If this is your desire, make it clear at the start of the interview. Some reporters may resist doing so. Therefore, make the request early on during the questioning. If the reporter is vehemently opposed, and threatens to write the story anyway, then ask the reporter to read back some of his/her notes. If the reporter has discombobulated your meaning, then you should either end the interview or again demand that the reporter read back the story before publication. If you cannot reach an agreement, contact the reporter's editor or news director.

4. Remember what you consider important and interesting may not be what whets the taste of the media and its audience. Because the press faces a space crunch, forcing the condensation and oversimplification of material, your life's work may be summarized in a few hundred words in print and a few short sentences on television. Be prepared for shock when a minor point in your work becomes the major thrust of the news article. To avert this result, ask the reporter before he leaves your office or lab to tell you what he thinks will be the focus of his story.

5. When talking to a reporter—even in a small town where the newspaper reaches only a few thousand people—remember that you may be reaching people thoughout the country, and possibly all over the world. The press is interwoven through wire services (the AP, UPI, Reuters, the N.Y. Times Service, and others). An interesting story in one community may "go out on the wires" to reach media throughout the world. The wire services get much of their news from subscribers, small radio stations, and newspapers in the hinterland of America. If you embellish claims about your small clinical study in rural Ortonville, but use words that make it sound significant, the press will accept that as gospel truth and send the message out to others, often without checking back with the scientist to confirm the accuracy of the original story. Once a story is disseminated through the wire services "it takes on a life of its own, disseminating with a velocity that makes it virtually impossible to retrieve and correct mistakes," writes Jeffrey Goldstein, chairman of the mass media committee for the International Society for Research on Aggression.[3]

6. Inquire about the reporter's credentials. Ask if he or she is a member of a professional association—the National Association of Science Writers or the American Medical Writers Association. Although membership, of course, will not guarantee accuracy, it is an indication that the reporter strives to be a professional, and takes some pride in his or her craft. If time permits, ask the reporter to submit writing samples before the interview.

7. Provide the reporter with plenty of background information, but don't overload the journalist with too many scientific articles. Supplement scientific journal papers with well-written pieces that have impressed you from popular magazines. Review articles are especially helpful to put new work into perspective.

8. Television creates special problems because of its brevity and reliance on pictures. Your story will last between thirty seconds and two minutes. To make sure your ideas are transmitted accurately, ask for a rehearsal before the lights go on. Some reporters will do this automatically. It gives you an opportunity to select the right words.

9. Be prepared for repercussions. If you're talking about any disease—even if it's basic research—many people will interpret the message, despite qualifiers, as a breakthrough. And they will call you wanting to participate in your study. Plan for the consumer barrage. If you work at a hospital, advise the switchboard of those expected inquiries. If you are unable to deal with patients' calls, be sure that someone—a social worker, nurse, or patient relations staffer—is available to answer questions. In the event of an avalanche of inquiries, which is inevitable if the research draws national coverage, prepare a form letter that corrects misunderstandings and offers guidance to patients who seek treatment.

10. If your patient decides to go public, suggest that the reporter's question about treatment and medications be deferred to you. Encourage the patient and the family to discuss only emotional, financial, and personal aspects of the case.

11. If the news report was in error, act quickly to correct it. First, notify the reporter and suggest that a correction be published as soon as possible (ask that it be read to you before publication). If you and the reporter cannot come to an agreement, then you have

the opportunity to write a letter-to-the-editor. Some television stations allow viewer response to their work, but it is much more difficult to gain that forum, and they are usually aired at odd hours.

APPENDIX **V** # The Right Time for Research News

When should information medical research be made public? Of the many points that divide medicine and the media (See Chapter 1), it is this question that probably triggers the most heated debate among reporters and scientists. Reaching a consensus would be the start of a bridge that would narrow the chasm between the two camps. In this chapter, we look at how America's leading medical journal deals with the dissemination of research results to the lay press.

## The NEJM Model

Pick up a newspaper on any Thursday morning and you are likely to find a story about medical research that was reported in "today's issue of the *New England Journal of Medicine.*" Published by the Massachusetts Medical Society with editors on staff of Harvard Medical School, the *Journal* is widely regarded by both physicians and journalists as one of the most prestigious medical journals in the world. "Having your work published in the *New England Journal of Medicine* is the equivalent of winning a mini-Nobel Prize in Medicine," says one university scientist.

Of the thousands of articles submitted to the *Journal* for review every year, only 10 to 13 percent are published. The *Journal* specializes in clinical medicine—research that is applicable to the actual needs of patients, as opposed to publishing basic research. Also, the *Journal* seeks to present information that has not been previously published in either a scientific journal or the lay press.

In recent years, the *Journal* has become *the* most widely quoted medical journal in the world by the lay press. Medical reporters subscribe and receive the *Journal* several days ahead of its Thursday publication date. But the material is embargoed, meaning that reporters are prohibited from releasing a story ahead of time; to do so, reporters run the risk of having their subscription cancelled.

## The Ingelfinger Rule

Though a popular source of medical news, the *Journal* news policy ires many reporters. Medical reporters anguish over the *Journal's* "Ingelfinger Rule," a dictum established by the late editor Franz J. Ingelfinger. Basically, the rule says that scientists who submit articles to the *Journal* are not to voluntarily release information about the work to the popular media prior to the time the work is published or rejected. At the same time, the *Journal* will not consider research that has been covered extensively in the popular press. Exempt from this rule is research that has an urgent public health impact, such as the discovery of dangerous toxins in the environment. Ingelfinger imposed the stipulation after seeing pieces of articles that were in press in the *Journal* appearing in "throwaway" medical magazines or in the popular press shortly before publication of the full article in his publication. The editor felt that the *Journal* had a right to protect its newsworthiness.[1]

Although Ingelfinger instituted the rule, Dr. Arnold S. Relman, *Journal* editor since 1977, has been forced to defend it during a period of aggressive press coverage of medicine. Relman has been criticized extensively by reporters who charge him with violating the rights of the press. A writer for the news section of *JAMA* once claimed that Relman was attempting to "restrict the free flow of medical news." Further, he called the Ingelfinger Rule a "form of prior restraint, not only unfair to the researcher involved, but a threat to medical reporters trying to gather and accurately disseminate news of medicine."[2]

Why such vehement language from journalists? The free press has a knee-jerk reaction to anything that resembles control over the right to publish information. Scientists who submit articles to journals may deny a reporter an interview or details about a study for fear that the news account will jeopardize his chance of being published.

Relman defends the Ingelfinger Rule on several counts. The

policy protects the scientific process by insuring that articles undergo intensive review, both by editors at the *Journal* and scientists at academic institutions who are familiar with the subject matter. Second, the policy allows practicing physicians a few days to review the *Journal* before it hits the lay press and, hence, the mass public. Doctors can be prepared in the event they have inquiries from patients who come questioning, "that new cure I read about in the newspaper."

Here's how Relman explained the rationale:

> We recognize that reporters are free to write about anything they want, but we take the position that it doesn't help the public, and it is detrimental to the profession (and to us as a medical journal, we admit) to have our stories published in the press before publication or even peer review. Such stories may be premature, incomplete, subject to revision and subject to gross misinterpretation.[3]

Not every journal has an Ingelfinger Rule. Some publications actively encourage press coverage of their research, publishing news releases simultaneously with the journal, in hopes of attracting the attention of the popular media.

## The Consensus Conference

From the consumer standpoint, when is the appropriate time to put your hope and trust in a new medical development? Although publication in a major scientific journal such as the *Journal*, *Science*, the *Lancet*, or the *Annals of Internal Medicine* means the work has undergone "peer review," that does not assure infallibility. In peer review, other scientists in the field have read the manuscript, looking for inconsistencies, and raising questions about methods.

But there is rarely an effort to duplicate the results; it is only a review. Fraudulent research results can—and have—slipped through the review process, and been picked up by the lay press for dissemination to the public. Also, honest research efforts can come to differing conclusions. For example, the October 24, 1985, issue of the *New England Journal of Medicine* carried two articles on the effect of giving female hormones to postmenopausal women. One study proved beyond a reasonable doubt that the hormones can "substantially" protect women against heart attacks, while the second study said hormones "substantially" increase their risk of having a heart attack. Both studies were carried out by respected scientists, both provided evidence to support their conclusions, and both passed the *Journal's* peer reviewers who could not detect a flaw in the methods of either study. Therefore, both articles were published with an accompanying editorial by one of the reviewers who wrote: "I simply cannot tell from the present evidence whether these hormones add to the risk of cardiovascular disease, diminish the risk, or leave it unchanged, and must resort to the investigator's great cop out: More research is needed."[4]

So, is there a valid source of information besides the medical journal that consumers can turn to for an accurate account of new research? The NIH Consensus Conference, where groups of experts pool their collective wisdom and decide the merits of a new procedure or new therapy, is one place to start. In recent years, NIH Consensus Conferences have discussed a variety of new treatments, ranging from organ transplantation to cystic fibrosis. To obtain information on the Consensus Conference statements, contact the NIH Public Information Office.

# References

## Introduction

1. Don Colburn, "How Media Cover Each Year's Disease of the Century," *Minneapolis Star & Tribune*, 22 February 1987.
2. R. Gordon Sheperd, "Selectivity of Sources: Reporting the Marijuana Controversy," *Journal of Communication* 31 (Spring 1981): 129–37.

## Chapter 1: Where Medicine and Media Clash

1. Daniel E. Koshland, Jr., "Scientific Literacy," *Science* 230 (1985): 391.
2. Quoted in: Barbara Gastel, *Presenting Science to the Public* (Philadelphia: ISI Press, 1983), 41.
3. Robert DuPont, "Coping with Controversial Research," in *Communicating University Research*, ed. Virginia C. Smith and Patricia L. Alberger (Washington, D.C.: Council for Advancement and Support of Education, 1985), 55.
4. Quoted in: Carol Tavris, "How to Publicize Science: A Case Study," in *Reporting Science: The Case of Aggression*, ed. Jeffrey H. Goldstein (Hillsdale, N.J.: Lawrence Erlbaum, 1986), 24.
5. Nancy Pfund and Laura Hofstadter, "Biomedical Innovation and the Press," *Journal of Communication* 31 (Spring 1981): 138–54.
6. David Shaw, "Science News: Experts See Distortions," *Los Angeles Times*, 13 January 1977.
7. Warren Leary, "How I Cover Science: Newspapers," in *Communicating University Research*, ed. Virginia C. Smith and Patricia L. Alberger (Washington, D.C.: Council for Advancement and Support of Education, 1985), 78.
8. Bill Symons, "Reporter Symons Replies," *Newsletter of the National Association of Science Writers* 30 (1982): 3–4.
9. Quoted in: Hillier Krieghbaum, *When Doctors Meet Reporters* (New York: New York University Press, 1957), 8.
10. Jo Ann Shroyer, "Careful Talk," *Minnesota Monthly*, February 1986, 44–46.
11. David Sutherland, personal communication with the author (RCH), 1981.
12. Lauren A. Woods, "Some Perspectives on Communication of Science to the General Public," in *Improving Information Exchange Between Scientists and*

*Representatives of the Communications Media: Conference II. Federation Proceedings* (1973): 1441–48.
13. "Herpes Drug Prevents the Spread of Shingles," *USA Today,* 16 June 1981.
14. *Science in the Streets* (New York: Twentieth Century Fund, 1984), 4.

**Chapter 2:** Media Constraints and Their Impact on Medical News

1. Franz J. Ingelfinger, "The General Medical Journal: For Readers or Repositories?" *New England Journal of Medicine* 296 (1977): 1258–64.
2. Ron Powers, "TV: The Sound and the Fury," *Gentleman's Quarterly,* December 1985, 90.
3. Warren Burkett, *News Reporting: Science, Medicine and High Technology* (Ames, IA: Iowa State University Press, 1986), 46.
4. Kristine Portnoy, "Medical News Reporting: Both Sides of the Story," *Michigan Medicine* 84 (1985): 32.
5. J. Albert Altschull, *Agents of Power: The Role of the News Media in Human Affairs* (New York: Annenberg/Longman Communication Books, 1984), 126.
6. Christine Russell et al., "How I Cover Science: Newspapers," in *Communicating University Research,* ed. Virginia C. Smith and Patricia L. Alberger (Washington, D.C.: Council for Advancement and Support of Education, 1985), 76–82.
7. Lee Goldman and Anita Loscalzo, "Fate of Cardiology Research Originally Published in Abstract Form," *New England Journal of Medicine* 303 (1980):255–59.
8. Arnold S. Relman, "News Reports of Medical Meetings: How Reliable Are the Abstracts?" *New England Journal of Medicine* 303 (1980): 277–78.
9. David Pearlman, "Informing the Public about Research: The Media," in *Communicating University Research,* ed. Virginia C. Smith and Patricia L. Alberger (Washington, D.C.: Council for Advancement and Support of Education, 1985), 70–75.
10. Katherine Lord, "Covering Medicine, Health: Four Special Challenges," in *Communicating Science and Research, Selected Articles from CASE Currents* (Washington, D.C.: Council for Advancement and Support of Education, 1979), 4–6.
11. Charles Petit, "Dartmouth's Big Story: How It Got Pumped Up and Then Deflated," *Newsletter of the National Association of Science Writers* 33 (1985): 1.

**Chapter 3:** Quackery, Flackery, and Hype

1. U.S. Congress, House Select Committee on Aging, *Quackery: A $10 Billion Scandal,* Report prepared by the Subcommittee on Health and Long-Term Care, 31 May 1984, Committee Publication No. 98–435.
2. Ibid, 1.

3. Stephan Barrett, "The Health Quack: Supersalesman of the Seventies," *Archives of Internal Medicine* 138 (1978): 1065–66.

4. *Health Quackery: Consumer's Union Report on False Health Claims, Worthless Remedies, and Unproved Therapies* (New York: Holt, Rinehart & Winston, 1980), 205.

5. *Quackery: A $10 Billion Scandal*, 33.

6. Robert M. Cunningham, Jr., "Of Snake Oil and Science," *Hospitals* 52 (1978): 79–82.

7. Warren Burkett, *News Reporting: Science, Medicine and High Technology* (Ames, IA: Iowa State University Press, 1986), 58.

8. "Doctors Seeking Patients Acquire Marketing Savvy," *St. Paul Pioneer Press*, 21 June 1983.

9. "Take the Initiative to Get Newspaper Coverage," *Medical World News*, 9 December 1985, 103.

10. Franz J. Ingelfinger, "The General Medical Journal: For Readers or Repositories," *New England Journal of Medicine* 296 (1977): 1258–64.

11. William Nolen, "Medical Zealots," *American Scholar* 56 (1987): 45–56.

12. Dana Johnson, "A Return to Snake Oil?" Presentation at the Department of Pediatrics Grand Rounds (Minneapolis, MN: University of Minnesota Hospital), 10 December 1986.

**Chapter 4:** Snake Venom and Multiple Sclerosis

1. Barry G.W. Arnason, "Multiple Sclerosis: Current Concepts and Mangement," *Hospital Practice* 17 (1982): 81–89.

2. Annabel Hecht, "Snake Venom: A Medicine? No Proof Yet," *FDA Consumer*, September 1981, 18–21.

3. Quoted in: "MS Group Under Pressure to Start Snake-Venom Trial," *Medical World News*, 10 December 1979, 33.

4. *FDA Consumer*, 19.

5. Constance Holden, "Flurry over Venom," *Science* 270 (1980): 161.

6. Victor M. Rivera et al., "Modified Snake Venom in Amyotrophic Lateral Sclerosis: Lack of Clinical Effectiveness," *Archives of Neurology* 37 (1980): 201.

7. Richard T. Johnson, "University Research: Medical and Life Sciences," in *Communicating University Research*, ed. Virginia C. Smith and Patricia L. Alberger (Washington, D.C.: Council for Advancement and Support of Education, 1985), 41–43.

8. Robert J. Slater and Alma C. Yearwood, "MS: Facts, Faith, and Hope," *American Journal of Nursing* 80 (1980): 276–81.

9. "Snake Venom Enjoined," *FDA Consumer*, June 1982, 4.

**Chapter 5:** A Dangerous Cure for Cystic Acne

1. Jim Sibbison, "Pushing New Drugs—Can the Press Kick the Habit," *Columbia Journalism Review* 24 (July/August 1985): 52–54.

2. "Stubborn and Vexing, That's Acne," *FDA Consumer,* May 1980, 14–15.

3. Gary L. Peck et al., "Prolonged Remissions of Cystic and Conglobate Acne with 13-Cis-Retinoic Acid," *New England Journal of Medicine* 300 (1979): 329–33.

4. "New Drug Approved for Acne," *New York Times,* 22 May 1982.

5. Claude S. Burton, Peter W. Eyre, and J. Lamar Callaway, "Acne and Accutane," *North Carolina Medical Journal* 45 (1984): 513.

6. "Accutane Alert: Birth Defects," *Harvard Medical School Health Letter* 11 (1986): 1.

7. Peter E. Pochi, "13-Cis-Retinoic Acid in Severe Acne," *New England Journal of Medicine* 300 (1979): 359–60.

8. "Acne—A Treatable Disease," *Harvard Medical School Health Letter* 4 (1979): 1–3.

9. "Three Women Give Birth to Deformed Babies," *New York Times,* 26 July 1983.

10. "Health Research Group Charges Acne Drug Accutane Is Oversold," *Washington Post,* 9 September 1983.

11. "Side Effects of Acne Drug Prompt Warning to Doctors," *New York Times,* 29 March 1984.

12. Edward J. Lammer et al., "Retinoic Acid Embryopathy," *New England Journal of Medicine* 313 (1985): 837–41.

13. Ronald C. Hansen and Robert A. Schwartz, "Use and Abuse of Accutane," *Arizona Medicine,* July 1983, 459–63.

**Chapter 6:** The Sulindac Seduction

1. Alan H. Wallace, "Publicity about Sulindac," *New England Journal of Medicine* 300 (1979): 734.

2. Cody Wasner and Brian Kotzin, "Sulindac 'Public Relations' Deplored," *New England Journal of Medicine* 300 (1979): 373.

3. Saeed Ahmad, Amjad I. Sheikh, and M.K. Meeran, "Publicity about Sulindac," *New England Journal of Medicine* 300 (1979), 374.

4. "New Arthritis Drug No Cure, Firm Says," *Washington Post,* 5 November 1978.

5. Alton Blakeslee, "Publicity about Sulindac," *New England Journal of Medicine* 300 (1979): 735.

6. Arnold S. Relman, "The Sulindac Story: What Is Medical News?" *New England Journal of Medicine* 300 (1979): 733–34.

**Chapter 7:** An "Apocryphal Tale" about Cerebral Palsy

1. Roger Witherspoon, "The Race Is Not to the Swift, Nor the Battle to Strong," *Atlanta Constitution,* 7 July 1979.

2. Roger Witherspoon, "Blacks and Health Care: A Question of Numbers," *Atlanta Constitution,* 21 July 1979.

3. Gail Dubrof, "Reverberations of a Hoax," *Atlanta Magazine,* December 1979, 126–28.

**Chapter 8:** Selenium Story Put Cystic Fibrosis Sufferers at Risk

1. Wayne Snodgrass, Barry H. Rumack, and John B. Sullivan, "Selenium: Childhood Poisoning and Cystic Fibrosis," *Clinical Toxicology* 18 (1981): 211–20.
2. Millie Nunemaker, "After 14 Years, Pryer, Courage and Wallach Diet Are Performing Wonder," *Hutchinson* (Kansas) *News*, 3 May 1979.
3. *National Health Federation Bulletin*, October 1979, 4–12.
4. Linda Shaw, "Selenium: Hope for Cystic Fibrosis?" *Prevention* 31 (October 1979): 122–30.
5. Morris Fishbein and Justin Fishbein, eds., *Fishbein's Illustrated Medical and Health Encyclopedia*, vol. 6 (Westport, CT: Stuttman, 1981), 780–83.
6. "Doctor Claims Cure for Cystic Fibrosis," *San Francisco Chronicle*, 3 December 1978.
7. Van S. Hubbard, Giulio Barbero, and H. Peter Chase, "Selenium and Cystic Fibrosis," *Journal of Pediatrics* 96 (1980): 421–22.

**Chapter 9:** Laetrile: Media Hype of Pseudoscience

1. Irving J. Lerner, "Laetrile: A Lesson in Cancer Quackery," *CA: A Cancer Journal for Clinicians* 31 (March/April 1981): 91–95.
2. "Laetrile: A Sure-Fire Argument," *Columbia Journalism Review* 16 (1978): 75–76.
3. "Debate over Laetrile," *Time*, 12 April 1971, 80.
4. Barbara J. Culliton, "Sloan-Kettering: The Trials of an Apricot Pit—1973," *Science* 182 (1973): 1000–03.
5. David Shaw, "Science News: Experts See Distortions," *Los Angeles Times*, 13 January 1977.
6. Transcript from evening news broadcast, produced by CBS News, 29 May 1975.
7. Zvi Fuks and Baruch Modan, "The Story of 'Joseph M'—Mass Media against Medical Bureaucracy," *Public Health Reports* 99 (1984): 338–42.
8. Robert W. Deniston, Rose Mary Romano, and Holly Keck, "Newspaper Coverage of Laetrile Clinical Trials Results," *Progress in Clinical and Biological Research* 130 (1983): 193–200.

**Chapter 10:** Cancer News Coverage

1. Vicki S. Freimuth et al., "Covering Cancer: Newspapers and the Public Interest," *Journal of Communication* 34 (1984): 62–73.
2. Robert W. Gerlach and Gerald P. Murphy, "Public Response to Cancer News: Analysis of Parade Article Response," *New York State Journal of Medicine* 78 (1978): 1309–13.
3. Steven A. Rosenberg et al., "Observations on the System Administration of Autologous Lymphokine-Activated Killer Cells and Recombinant Interleuken-2 to Patients with Metastatic Cancer," *New England Journal of Medicine* 313 (1985): 1485–92.

4. "Doctors Urge Caution on Cancer Therapy," *Dallas Morning News*, 9 December 1985.

5. Mary Alice Williams, "Media and Medicine" (Address presented at the opening of the new University of Minnesota Hospital, 11 February 1986).

6. Charles G. Moertel, "On Lymphokines, Cytokines, and Breakthroughs," *Journal of the American Medical Association* 256 (1986): 3141.

7. Ron Kotulak, "False Hopes Cloud Cancer Achievements," *Chicago Tribune*, 22 December 1985.

8. Alan R. Feinstein, D.M. Sosin, and Carolyn K. Wells, "The Will Rogers Phenomenon: Stage Migration and New Diagnostic Techniques as a Source of Misleading Statistics for Survival in Cancer," *New England Journal of Medicine* 312 (1985): 1604–08.

9. John C. Bailar and Elaine M. Smith, "Progress against Cancer," *New England Journal of Medicine* 314 (1986): 1226–32.

10. Jane Brody, "Strange, Cancer-like Ailment Turns out to Be a New Disease," *New York Times*, 4 January 1983.

11. Walter Parker, "Medical Sleuthing Opens New Skin-Cancer Hope," *St. Paul Dispatch*, 19 July 1982.

12. Kevin J. Flynn et al., "Regressing Atypical Histiocytosis: A Cutaneous Proliferation of Atypical Neoplastic Histiocytes with Unexpectedly Indolent Biological Behavior," *Cancer* 49 (1982): 959–70.

13. Kevin J. Flynn, personal communication with author (RCH), 1983.

**Chapter 11:** Herpes Hysteria

1. Henry H. Balfour, Jr., and Ralph C. Heussner, *Herpes Diseases and Your Health* (Minneapolis: University of Minnesota Press, 1984), 3–5.

2. Lata S. Nerurkar et al., "Survival of Herpes Simplex Virus in Water Specimens Collected from Hot Tubs in Spa Facilities and on Plastic Surfaces," *Journal of the American Medical Association* 250 (1983): 3081–83.

3. John M. Douglas and Lawrence Corey, "Fomites and Herpes Simplex Virus: A Case for Nonvenereal Transmission?" *Journal of the American Medical Association* 250 (1983): 3093–94.

4. Jon Van, "Herpes Virus Found to Survive on Hot Tub Benches," *Chicago Tribune*, 9 December 1983.

5. Richard Lyon, "Health Officials Report Herpes Surge in Newborns," *New York Times*, 9 December 1983.

6. Transcript from evening news broadcast, produced by NBC News, 8 December 1983.

7. George J. Pazin and James H. Harger, "Transmission of Herpes Simplex," *Journal of the American Medical Association* 252 (1984): 1010–11.

8. Victor Cohn, "Herpes Virus Can Contaminate Hot Tub Areas, Journal Says," *Washington Post*, 9 December 1983.

9. Transcript from "Children with Herpes," produced by ABC News, 14 January 1985.

10. Transcript from "Children with Herpes: How Great the Danger?" produced by ABC News, 11 January 1985.

**Chapter 12:** Acupuncture and Hearing Loss

1. Alfred Peng, "Acupuncture Treatment for Deafness: A Preliminary Report," *American Journal of Chinese Medicine* (1973): 155–58.
2. David N. F. Fairbanks, Ellis A. Wallenberg, and Blair M. Webb, "Acupuncture for Hearing Loss," *Archives of Otolaryngology* 99 (1974): 395–401.
3. *Ibid.*
4. S.M. Abel, H.O. Barber, and T.D.R. Briant, "A Study of Acupuncture in Adult Sensorineural Hearing Loss," *Journal of Otolaryngology* 6 (1977): 166–71.

**Chapter 13:** The Vasectomy Scare

1. Nancy J. Alexander and Thomas B. Clarkson, "Vasectomy Increases the Severity of Diet-Induced Atherosclerosis in Macaca Fascicularies," *Science* 201 (1978): 538–41.
2. "Vasectomy-Cholesterol Study Viewed at Fertility Society Meeting," *Washington Post*, 1 April 1978.
3. Boyce Bensenger, "Monkey Vasectomies Hint Harm to Artery," *New York Times*, 1 April 1978.
4. Robert Benjamin, personal communication with author (RCH), 1985.
5. Quoted in: "Quick Cut Straight to the Heart," *Macleans*, 3 October 1980, 58.
6. M.J. Goldacre, T.R. Holford, and M.P. Vessey, "Cardiovascular Disease and Vasectomy: Findings from Two Epidemiologic Studies," *New England Journal of Medicine* 308 (1983): 805–8.

**Chapter 14:** Sweet News for Diabetics?

1. John P. Bartle et al., "Postprandial Glucose and Insulin Responses to Meals Containing Different Carbohydrates in Normal and Diabetic Subjects," *New England Journal of Medicine* 309 (1983): 7–12.
2. David M. Nathan et al., "Ice Cream in Diet of Insulin-Dependent Diabetic Patients," *Journal of the American Medical Association* 251 (1981): 2825–27.
3. Steven Findlay, "Sugar: Study OKs It for Diabetics," *USA Today*, 7 July 1983.
4. John P. Bartle, transcript from news conference, 7 July 1983.
5. David J. A. Jenkins, "Dietary Carbohydrates and Their Glycemic Responses," *Journal of the American Medical Association* 251 (1984): 2829–31.

**Chapter 15:** Whooping Cough Makes a Comeback

1. Joseph H. Bloom, "Is Whooping Cough Making a Comeback?" *Newssearch*, September 1986, 3.

2. "Pertussis," *Taber's Cyclopedia Medical Directory* (Philadelphia: F.A. Davis, 1971), 43.

3. Marjorie Sun, "Whooping Cough Vaccine Research Revs Up," *Science* 227 (1985): 1184–86.

4. Christopher L. Cody et al., "Nature and Rates of Adverse Reactions Associated with DPT and DT Immunizations in Infants and Children," *Pediatrics*, November 1981, 650–59.

5. Quoted in: Lois Wingerson and Mark Bloom, "Did DPT Get Smeared on National Television?" *Medical World News*, 7 June 1982, 30–32.

6. *Ibid.*

7. Vincent A. Fulginiti, "Campaign of Terror—Comment," *American Journal of Diseases in Children* 137 (1983): 923.

8. Oliver Gillie, "Vaccines: What Every Parent Needs to Know," (London) *Sunday Times*, 13 June 1976.

9. Geoffrey Edsall, "A Little Learning," (London) *Sunday Times*, 20 June 1976.

10. "Vaccine Call Is Attacked," (London) *Sunday Times*, 26 June 1977.

11. "Father Says Vaccine Killed Son," (London) *Times*, 25 April 1978.

12. David L. Miller and Euan M. Ross, "Whooping Cough: A Shot in the Dark," *British Medical Journal* 286 (1983): 1817–18.

**Chapter 16:** Pinwheel Surgery Controversy

1. Tutomu Sato, Koichiro Akiyama, and Hirohiko Shibata, "A New Surgical Approach to Myopia," *American Journal of Opthalmology* 36 (1953): 823–29.

2. "Radial Keratotomy," *Harvard Medical School Health Letter* 6 (1980): 6.

3. Marjorie Sun, "Institute, Keratotomists Don't See Eye to Eye," *Science* 2213 (1981): 423–24.

4. "Far Out Surgery for the Nearsighted," *Columbus* (Ohio) *Evening Dispatch*, 5 June 1983.

5. Virginia Rybin, "Experimental Surgery Raises Hopes for Nearsighted," *St. Paul Pioneer Press*, 22 March 1981.

6. "Jury Still Out on Keratotomy," *Medical World News*, 12 May 1986, 88.

7. "Update on Surgery for Nearsightedness," *Harvard Medical School Health Letter* 10 (1985): 4.

**Chapter 17:** AIDS

1. Ron Kotulak, "AIDS Victim Improves: Drug Gets More Tests," *Chicago Tribune*, 10 February 1985.

2. Matt Clark et al., "AIDS Exiles in Paris," *Newsweek*, 5 August 1985, 71.

3. Darrel Y. Rist, "The French Connection," *New York Post*, 14 September 1985.

4. David Pearlman, "Experts Discount French Report on New AIDS Drug," *San Francisco Chronicle*, 3 October 1985.

**Chapter 18:** The Charity Campaigns

1. Lisa Levitt, "Dying Kids Can Live—But Who Will Bear Costs?" *St. Paul Pioneer Press*, 10 July 1983.

2. David Wessel, "Transplants Increase, and So Do Disputes Over Who Pays Bills," *Wall Street Journal*, 12 April 1984.
3. Joan Beck, "Facing Agony of Transplant Decisions," *St. Paul Pioneer Press*, 28 March 1983.
4. Phil Gunby, "Media-Abetted Liver Transplants Raise Questions of 'Equity and Decency,' " *Journal of the American Medical Association* 249 (1983): 973–1982.

**Chapter 19:** Media Promotes an "Inebriated Nation"

1. Lewis Cope, "Liquor Industry's Ads Called 'Program for Inebriated Nation,' " *Minneapolis Star & Tribune*, 30 May 1984.
2. Donald E. Strickland, "Alcohol Advertising: Content and Controversy," *Journal of Advertising* 1 (1982): 223–36.
3. "Alcohol: Advertising, Counteradvertising, and Depiction in the Public Media," *Journal of the American Medical Association* 256 (1986): 1485–88.
4. *Ibid.*
5. "Omnibus Petition for Regulation of Unfair and Deceptive Alcoholic Beverage Advertising and Marketing Practices," (Washington, D.C.: Center for Science in the Public Interest, 1985).

**Chapter 20:** Tobacco Industry's "Switch to Print" Pays Off

1. William U. Chandler, "Banishing Tobacco," *Worldwatch Paper #68* (Washington, D.C.: Worldwatch Institute, 1986), p. 5.
2. "Media Advertising for Tobacco Products," *Journal of the American Medical Association* 255 (1986): 1033.
3. Elizabeth M. Whelan et al., "Analysis of Coverage of Tobacco Hazards in Women's Magazines," *Journal of Public Health Policy* 2 (1981): 28–35.
4. Elizabeth M. Whelan, "When *Newsweek* and *Time* Filtered Cigarette Copy," *Wall Street Journal*, 1 November 1984.
5. R.C. Smith, "The Magazines' Smoking Habit," *Columbia Journalism Review* 16 (1978): 29–31.
6. "New Medium for the Message," *Consumer Reports* 41 (May 1976): 277–79.
7. "Notes and Comment," *New Yorker*, 27 June 1976, 23–24.

**Chapter 21:** Suicides and the "Power of Suggestion"

1. Billy Williams, personal communication with author (RCH), 1973.
2. "Television News and Imitation Suicides: The Power of Suggestion," *Hastings Center Report* 13 (April 1983): 3.
3. David P. Phillips and Lundie L. Carstensen, "Clustering of Teenage Suicides after Television News Stories about Suicide," *New England Journal of Medicine* 315 (1986): 685–89.
4. Madelyn S. Gould and David Shaffer, "The Impact of Suicide in Television Stories," *New England Journal of Medicine* 315 (1986): 390–94.
5. Leon Eisenberg, "Does Bad News about Suicide Beget Bad News?" *New England Journal of Medicine* 315 (1986): 705–6.

6. *Vital Statistics: A Memorial Volume of Selections from the Reports and Writings of William Farr,* ed. Noel A. Humphreys (Metuchen, NJ: Scarecrow Press, 1975), 301–2.

**Chapter 24:** A Consumer's Guide to Medical News and Advertising.

1. Wayne L. Pines, "A Primer on New Drug Development," *FDA Consumer,* February 1974, 12–18.

**Chapter 25:** What to Do about Quackery

1. U.S. Congress, House Select Committee on Aging, *Quackery: A $10 Billion Scandal,* Report prepared by the Subcommittee on Health and Long-Term Care, 31 May 1984, Committee Publication No. 98–435.
2. *Ibid,* 196.

**Appendix III:** A Reporter's Notebook

1. Victor Cohn, "Media and Medicine" (Address presented at the opening of the new University of Minnesota Hospital, 11 February 1986).
2. David Cassady, "Press Councils—Why Journalists Won't Cooperate," *Newspaper Research Journal* 5 (1984): 19–25.

**Appendix IV:** Rx for Medical People

1. William Osler, "Internal Medicine as a Vocation," *Aequanimitas, with Other Addresses to Medical Students, Nurses and Practitioners of Medicine* (London: H.K. Lewis, 1906).
2. Phillip J. Tichenor et al., "Mass Communications Systems and Communication Accuracy in Science News Reporting," *Journalism Quarterly* 47 (1970): 673–83.
3. Jeffrey Goldstein, *Handbook for Science Communication* (International Society for Research on Aggression, 1985), 10.

**Appendix V:** The Right Time for Research News

1. Franz J. Ingelfinger, "Definition of 'Sole Contribution,'" *New England Journal of Medicine* 28 (1969): 676–77.
2. John Elliott, "Relman of NEJM Accused of Restricting Free Flow of News," *Newsletter of the National Association of Science Writers* 28 (1979): 5.
3. Arnold S. Relman, "The Relationship Between Medicine and the Press—A Panel Discussion," *Pharos,* Summer 1981, 31.
4. John C. Bailar, III, "When Research Results Are in Conflict," *New England Journal of Medicine* 33 (1985): 1080–81.

# Index

ABC-TV, 55, 98–99, 159–60
Accuracy, x, 10–11, 200
Accutane, 53–61
Acne, 53–61
Acquired Immune Deficiency
    Syndrome (*See* AIDS)
Acupuncture, 100–104
Acyclovir, 13
Advertising, xi, 34–39, 125, 179–82
    of alcohol, 145–49
    of tobacco, 150–57
AIDS, 22, 129–34, 194
AIDS Medical Foundation, 130
Alcohol, 145–49, 194
Alexander, Nancy, 105–106
Altschull, J. Albert, 20
Alzheimer's disease, 18, 26, 33, 192,
    194
American College of Hospital
    Administrators, 42
American Council on Science and
    Health, 151
American Diabetes Association, 113,
    115
*American Journal of Chinese Medicine,*
    100
*American Journal of Nursing,* 51
American Medical Association, 39,
    146–48, 150
American Medical Writers
    Association, 201
American Psychiatric Association, 4
Amyotrophic lateral sclerosis, 49–50
Animal research, 28–31, 105–109, 184
AP (*See* Associated Press)
Appeal stories, 140
*Archives of Internal Medicine,* 33
Archives of Neurology, 50
Argot, 10

*Arizona Medicine,* 60
Arthritis, 16, 33–36, 45–46, 62–67
Aspirin, 66
Associated Press, 6, 24, 54–56, 63,65,
    67, 126, 137, 200
*Atlanta Constitution,* 68–70
*Atlanta Journal,* 158
Atlanta Magazine, 68–69

Baby Fae, 18
Bantle, John P., 112, 114
Barbero, Giulio, 76
Barrett, Stephan, 33–34
Beck, Joan, 141
Benjamin, Robert, 107
Bigley, Johnny, 98
Biliary atresia, 138
Biomedical revolution, ix
Blakeslee, Alton, 65–66
Blindness, 53, 194
Bloom, Mark, 118
Booth, Jennifer, 137
Breakthrough, 5, 41, 67, 80, 87, 89,
    114, 117, 131, 134, 188, 201
*British Medical Journal,* 121
Brody , Jane, 19
Brokaw, Tom, 96
Burkett, Warren, 19, 38
*Business Week,* 123

*Cancer,* 92
Cancer news coverage, 78–92, 136, 194
Cassady, David, 198
Catalyst Altered Water, 35
Cataracts, 124
CBS-TV, 18, 45, 47, 55, 82, 160
CDC (*See* Centers for Disease Control)
Censorship, 77

Center for Science in the Public
  Interest, 145, 148
Centers for Disease Control, 97–98,
  118
Cerebral palsy, 68–70
Chase, Peter, 76
Checkbook journalism, 176
Chemotherapy, 28
Chermann, Jean-Claude, 131
*Chicago Daily News*, 8
*Chicago Tribune*, 89, 95, 97, 131, 141
Cholesterol, 105
Chubbuck, Christine, 159
Cigarettes, 150–56
Clinoril (*See* Sulindac)
Code of Cooperation, 8
Cohn, Victor, 19, 196
*Columbia Journalism Review*, 54
*Columbus* (Ohio) *Evening Dispatch*, 125
Communications process, 16–18
Competition, 9–10, 16, 20, 25, 39, 42
Consensus conference, 76, 205–206
*Consumer Reports*, 34, 156
Controversy, 10, 23, 79, 118, 123–28,
  145
Cooke, Janet, 70
Cope, Lewis, 19
Corey, Lawrence, 95
*Cosmopolitan*, 151
*Current Therapy*, 182
Cyclosporine, 130, 133–34
Cystic fibrosis, 72–77,

Deadlines, 6, 27–31
Deafness, 5, 100–104
*Denver Post*, 7
*Des Moines Register*, 70
*Detroit News*, 20, 123
DeVries, William, 27
Diabetes, 110–15, 194
Diets, 34, 72–76, 110–15
DNA, 5
Douglas, John M., 95
DPT vaccine, 116
Drugs
  Accutane, 53–61
  Acyclovir, 13
  Cyclosporine, 130, 133–34
    effects, 12, 39
  HPA-23, 130–32, 134
  Interferon, 31

Interleukin-2, 87, 130
  process of approval, 184–86
Laetrile, 78–84
  marketing of, 33–35
Penicillamine, 64
Phenylbutazone, 65–66
PROven, 45–52
  side effects, 55, 59, 63
Sulindac, 62–67
Thalidomide, 57
Dubrof, Gail, 69–70
Dupont, Robert, 4

East, John, 159
Edsall, Geoffrey, 120
Eisenberg, Leon, 162
Embargo, 111, 203
End Stage Renal Disease (ESRD)
  program, 139
Epidemiology, 107, 118
Escalambre, Rachel, 136–37
*Esquire*, 34
Experimental, 11, 125, 130, 138–39
Experts, 13

*Family Circle*, 151
Farr, William, 162
FDA (*See* Food and Drug
  Administration)
*FDA Consumer*, 184
Federal Communications
  Commission, (FCC), 155
Federal Trade Commission, (FTC),
  35–36, 146, 148–49, 189
Flackery, 38
Flynn, Kevin J., 91–92
Foege, William H., 118
Food and Drug Administration,
  (FDA), 7, 35–36, 45, 48–50, 53, 55–56,
  58, 62, 64, 78, 118, 184–85, 187–88,
  191
Fuks, Zvi, 82
Fulginiti, Vincent A., 119

Gatekeepers, 16
Gerlach, Robert W., 86
Gillie, Oliver, 120
Glaucoma, 124
Goldman, Lee, 22
Goldstein, Jeffrey, 200

*Good Housekeeping,* 151–52, 154
Gould, Madelyn S., 161

Haast, William, 45–48
Hansen, Ronald C., 60
Harger, James H., 97
*Harper's Bazaar,* 151
*Harvard Medical School Health Letter,* 57, 124
Haseltine, Nathan S., 10
Health maintenance organization, 42
Health Research Group, 58
Hearing loss, 100–104
Hemophilia, 130
Herpes, 13, 33, 93–99
Hersh, Evan, 88
Hoffman-La Roche, 53, 56, 58
Hofstadter, Laura, 5
Holmes, Oliver Wendell, 33
Homosexuality, 4
Hospice, 42
*Hospital Index,* 181
*Houston Post,* 131
HPA-23, 23, 130–32, 134
Hubbard, Van S., 76
Hucksterism, 37
Hudson, Rock, 132
*Hutchinson* (Kansas) *News,* 73
Hydrocephalus, 7
Hype, 32, 37, 40–1

*Index Medicus,* 47, 181, 188, 197
Informants, 16
Ingelfinger, Franz J., 15, 40
Interferon, 31
Interleukin-2, 87, 130
Investigational drugs, 184–86
Isotretinoin (*See* Accutane)

Jacobson, Michael F., 145
*JAMA* (See *Journal of American Medical Association*)
Jenkins, David J.A., 114
Johnson, Dana, 42
Johnson, Richard T., 50
Journal articles, 183
*Journal of American Medical Association,* 89, 94–97, 111, 113, 142, 204
*Journal of Communication,* 5
*Journal of Pediatrics,* 76

*Journal of Public Health Policy,* 151

Kaiser-Permanente, 136
Kehoe, Joe, 82
Koppel, Ted, 98–99
Kotulak, Ron, 89
Kotzin, Brian, 64
Krebs, Ernst, 78
Krebs, Ernst, Jr., 78–79

*Ladies Home Journal,* 151
Laetrile, 78–84
*Lancet,* 132
Language barriers, 10–12
Lead, 30
Leary, Warren, 6
Legionnaires' disease, ix
LeRiche, Roy, 101
Leukemia, 31
Levitt, Lisa, 137
Leyden, James, 55
*London Times,* 120–21
*Los Angeles Times,* 81–82
Loscalzo, Anita, 22

*Mademoiselle,* 151
Mail order, 35
Marketing, 37–39
Mayer, Robert, 88
Mayo Clinic, 83, 89, 192
McCall's, 151
McNare, Donje, 137–39
Medelsohn, Robert, 193
Mediagenic, 140–41
Medical
    evangelists, 40, 134
    journals, 23, 183
    meetings, 21, 108
    zealots, 41
*Medical World News,* 39, 48
Medicalese, 27, 135
MEDLARS, 22
MEDLINE, 182
Mental illness, 4
Merck, 62, 65, 67
*Merck Manual,* 182
*Miami Herald,* 131
Miller, David L., 121
*Minneapolis Star & Tribune,* 19
Minnesota Public Radio, 11

Mob journalism, 25
Modan, Baruch, 82
Moertel, Charles G., 83, 89
Monroe, Marilyn, 159
Montagnier, Luc, 130-31
*Mother Jones*, 152
Multiple sclerosis, 45-52
Murphy, Gerald P., 86
Myopia, 123

National Arthritis Foundation, 63
National Association of Science
    Writers, 201
National Cancer Information Service,
    87
National Cancer Institute, 55, 83, 85,
    87
National Eye Institute, 124
*National Geographic*, 156
*National Health Federation Bulletin*, 73
National Institutes of Health, 76,
    94-96, 124, 184, 192-93, 206
*National Leader*, 138
National Multiple Sclerosis Society,
    49, 51
National News Council, 80, 197-98
NBC-TV, 55, 57, 88, 96-97, 116, 160
Nearsightedness, 123-24
Nelson, Harry, 81
Nerurkar, Lata S., 96
Neuroblastoma, 136
*New England Journal of Medicine*, 15, 22,
    40, 59, 64, 66, 87, 90, 111, 160, 203
*New York Post*, 131
*New York Times*, 15, 20, 58, 91, 96-97,
    101, 106, 108, 131, 180, 200
*New Yorker*, 154, 156
Newhouse News Service, 20
News
    conference, 17, 25, 60, 112
    council, 80, 197-98
    release, 17, 24, 62, 67
*Newsletter of the National Association of
    Science Writers*, 26
*Newsweek*, 45, 48, 60, 87, 101, 123, 129,
    153
"Nightline," 98-99
NIH (*See* National Institutes of Health)
Nossal, Gustav, 107
Nostrums, 32

Objectivity, 4-5, 18-20, 38, 67, 126, 169
Organ transplantation, 135-39,
    141-42, 175-76
Osler, William, 199
Otolaryngology, 102

Pack mentality, 22
Panacea, 101
Pancreas, 11, 110
*Parade*, 86
Pasteur Institute, 130
Patient package insert, 57
Pazin, George J., 97
Pearlman, David, 19, 23
Peck, Gary L., 55-56
Peer review, 4, 6, 23-25, 205
Peng, Alfred, 100-03
Pennsylvania Medical Society, 34
Pepper, Claude, 189
Pertussis (*See* Whooping cough)
Petit, Charles, 26
Pfund, Nancy, 5
Phenylbutazone, 65-66
Phillips, David P., 160, 162
*Physician's Desk Reference*, 182
Placebo, 27, 36, 48
Play, 10, 20
Pochi, Peter E., 57
Polio, 6, 46
Powers, Ron, 18
Press release (*See* news release)
*Prevention*, 73
Prinze, Freddie, 159
Privacy, 8, 27, 136, 174-76
Promotion, 16
Propaganda, 156-57
PROven, 45
"Pseudo-cancers," 91-92
Pseudoscience, 78
Public Health Service, 162
Public relations, 17, 24, 26, 38-39, 62,
    65, 174, 180
Pulitzer Prize, 70

Quackery, 4, 19, 32, 50, 83, 98, 187-89
Qualifiers, 12-23, 111-12

Radial keratotomy, 123
RAH (*See* Regressing Atypical
    Histiocytosis)

Readback policy, 196, 200
*Reader's Digest*, 154, 156
*Redbook*, 151
Regressing Atypical Histiocytosis, 91–92
Relman, Arnold S., 22, 66, 204–05
Reuters, 200
Rosenbaum, Sarah, 140
Rosenberg, Steven, 88
Rozenbaum, Willy, 131

Saccharin, 156
*St. Paul Dispatch*, 92
*St. Paul Pioneer Press*, 126
Salk, Jonas, 6
*San Francisco Chronicle*, 19, 23, 131, 134
*San Francisco Examiner*, 137
Sarett, Lewis H., 62
Sato, Tutomu, 124
Savitch, Jessica, 55
*Science*, 3, 81
*Science in the Streets*, 14
Scientific method, 5
Scientists' Institute for Public Information, 130
Scoop journalism, 9, 170
Selenium, 72–77, 188
Semantics, 10–12, 59–60
Sensationalism, x, 3, 5, 62, 116, 173
*Seventeen*, 151
Shaffer, David, 161
Shepherd, R. Gordon, x
Sheppard, Ben, 45–48
Shingles, 13
Shroyer, Jo Ann, 11
Sibbison, Jim, 54
"60 Minutes," 35, 45, 47–48, 50
*Sky*, 47
Slater, Robert J., 51
Smith, Elaine M., 90
Smith, R.C., 153–54
Snake venom, 45–52
Sources, 13–14, 99
*Sports Illustrated*, 34
Strait, George, 55
Straus, Stephen, 98
Suicide, 158–63
Sulindac, 62–67
Sullivan, Walter, 20

Surgeon general, 149–50

Taylor, Samuel G., 80
Testimonials, 26, 51, 79, 82
Thalidomide, 57
Tichenor, Phillip J., 199
*Time*, 81, 153
Timeliness, 5
Tobacco, 150–56
Toxic shock syndrome, ix
Transplants (*See* organ transplantation)
Twain, Mark, vii

Ulcers, 23
United Press International (UPI), 55–56, 63, 67, 73, 74, 101, 126, 200
*USA Today*, 13, 112

Vaccines, 116–22
Vasectomy, 105–109
Victimization, 172
Vitamins
Vitamin A, 56, 58
Vitamin B17, 79
*Vogue*, 151
von Goethe, Johann Wolfgang, 159
Voyeurism, 167–73

Waksman, Byron, 48–49
*Wall Street Journal*, 153
Wallace, Alan H., 64
Wallach, Joel, 73–76
*Washington Post*, 10, 19, 26, 34, 70, 97, 106, 108, 180, 196
Wasner, Cody, 64
Whelan, Elizabeth M., 151, 153
Whiteside, Thomas, 154
Whooping cough, 116–22
*Who's Who in Medicine*, 182
Williams, Billy, 158–59
Winsten, Jay, viii
Witherspoon, Roger, 68–71
*Woman's Day*, 151
Woods, Lauren A., 12
WRC-TV, 116

Yerkes Primate Research Center, 73
Young, Patrick, 20